W9-ANY-341

THE CHALLENGING DREAM
OF HEART SURGERY

From the Pampas to Cleveland

THE CHALLENGING DREAM OF HEART SURGERY

From the Pampas to Cleveland

René G. Favaloro, M.D.

Little, Brown and Company
Boston/New York/Toronto/London

Copyright © 1994 by René G. Favaloro

All rights reserved. No part of this book may be
reproduced in any form or by any electronic or
mechanical means, including information storage
and retrieval systems, without permission in
writing from the publisher, except by a reviewer
who may quote brief passages in a review.

Library of Congress Cataloging-in-Publication Data

Favaloro, René G., 1923-
  [De la pampa a los Estados Unidos. English]
  The challenging dream of heart surgery : from the Pampas to
Cleveland / René G. Favaloro. -- 1st ed.
    p.   cm.
  Translated from Spanish by Peter Willshaw.
  ISBN 0-316-26026-6
  1. Favaloro, René G., 1923-   . 2. Surgeons--Argentina--
Biography. 3. Coronary heart disease--Surgery--Ohio--Cleveland--
History. 4. Cleveland Clinic Foundation. I. Title.
  [DNLM:1. Favaloro, René G., 1923-   . 2. Heart Surgery--personal
narratives. 3. Coronary Arteriosclerosis--surgery--personal
narratives. WZ 100 F7272 1994a]
RD598.F3813 1994
617.4'12059'092--dc20
[B]
DNLM/DLC
for Library of Congress   93-36345
                                                   CIP

Printed in the United States of America
RRD-VA

Editorial: Thomas Manning
Production Supervisor/Designer: Madeline Belliveau
Cover Designer: Madeline Belliveau

Dedication

This book is dedicated to the memory of Mason Sones.

In "Life Without Principle" Henry David Thoreau wrote: *Even the facts of science may dust the mind by their dryness, unless they are in a sense effaced each morning, or rather rendered fertile by the dews of fresh and living truth.*

I do not have any doubt that in addition to his outstanding contribution to modern cardiology Mason was always thoroughly searching for the *living truth* following strict ethical rules. His *fertile* mind was ready to share with us knowledge and friendship. He had no need to *efface any dust* because *the facts of his science* were the consequence of an honest life.

Contents

A. Experimental work
B. Clinical application of aortocoronary bypass
C. Experimental work on mammary coronary anastomosis
D. Clinical application of internal mammary artery

Foreword

Most autobiographic accounts bear scant resemblance to fact, regardless of the author's intent. Fading memory, self-justification, vanity, subsequent experiences in life and sometimes a desire to shock the reader tend to distort the tale. René G. Favaloro's devotion to truth should be evident even to the reader who is unacquainted with him personally. From a decade of close and almost daily contact with him, I can verify much of the factual account and the remainder I accept on faith because of his unvarnished honesty. A second theme running through the book and evident to those with whom he has worked is the best possible care of the patient at hand, as well as patients in general. Nothing that can be improved is good enough. He treats the patient as well as the disease and patients respond. In honesty and care of the patient he is like his late and good friend, Mason Sones.

The third principle governing René's professional life is dedication to teaching. In a way this is related to the second theme because by teaching a master physician passes on to students both knowledge and dedication to patient care.

René Favaloro is well read in history and the classics. One of his favorite books is *Don Quixote* and some have thought that he bears a resemblance to the principal character. This analogy is apt insofar as it applies to struggle towards the ideal. When we were preparing for anatomical dissection in medical school, our brilliant lecturer said, "Gentlemen, man is a soul, he has a body." Don Quixote would have endorsed that belief and Dr. René G. Favaloro has lived by it. Although he is loyal to his Catholic Church, his Italian heritage, and his native country, he is respectful to and loves those of other faiths and nationalities. It is fitting that he spent long years as a general surgeon in a remote and poor area of Argentina ministering to people who were largely Protestants or Jews. He looked on them as souls with sick bodies and they regarded him as a friend and dedicated physician. This book is a sequel to that story but the man is the same.

William L. Proudfit, M.D.
Emeritus Consultant
Department of Cardiology
Cleveland Clinic Foundation

Preface

This book describes the development of important steps in the understanding and surgical treatment of coronary arteriosclerosis, the most frequent cause of disability and death at present. I have tried to use language which avoids technical expressions but believe that at the outset the reader should refresh his or her knowledge of the anatomy and blood supply of the heart to make it easier to understand the message I wish to convey.

The heart is a specialized muscle that contracts rhythmically to pump the blood into the system of blood vessels. The blood returns to the right atrium of the heart by way of the vascular system (Figure 1). The inferior vena cava carries most of the blood returned from the body, and the superior vena cava contributes blood mainly from the head, neck, and upper extremities. From the right atrium the blood passes into the right ventricle through the tricuspid valve. The contraction of the right ventricle forces the blood into the pulmonary artery which conveys it to both lungs. In the lungs it is reoxygenated through the delicate walls of the pulmonary alveoli (air sacs), changing its color from blue to red. It returns to the heart by way of the pulmonary veins after passing through the microscopically small capillary vessels, and drains into the left atrium - which is medial and posterior as our professor, Galli, would always remind us, due to its being located midway between the lungs. From the left atrium it passes into the left ventricle through the mitral valve. This ventricle has thick muscular walls which contract to force the blood through the entire body via the aorta and its branches.

As we have seen, the heart consists of muscle which has some special properties due to the fact that it does not rest for long in each cardiac cycle. It works day and night to

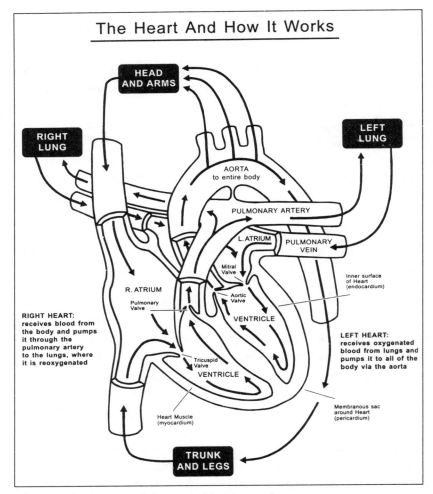

Fig. 1. *The heart and the main blood vessels.*

keep us alive, and for this reason its nutritional needs are great. Of all the organs, it is the heart that extracts most oxygen from the blood flowing through it.

This blood is delivered to the heart muscle via the coronary arteries. There are two main arteries, the left and the right (Figure 2). Both originate in the initial part of the ascending aorta. The right coronary artery proceeds from the anterior wall of the aorta, coursing in the groove between

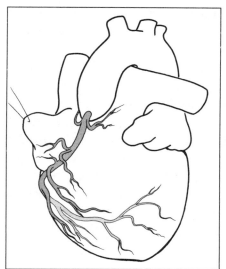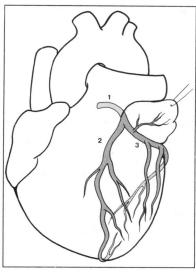

Fig. 2A. *Right Coronary artery distribution.*

Fig. 2B. *Left coronary artery distribution.*
1. Left main coronary trunk.
2. Anterior descending branch.
3. Circumflex branch.

the right atrium and right ventricle to reach the posterior or diaphragmatic wall where it divides into various branches.It irrigates the right atrium, the right ventricle, and part of the interventricular septum; when the artery is large (what we refer to as a dominant right coronary), it can reach as far as the posterior or diaphragmatic wall of the left ventricle.

The left coronary artery originates in the internal posterior part of the aorta and passes behind the pulmonary artery. Its main trunk soon divides into two branches. The anterior descending artery lies in the groove between the two ventricles and through its branches supplies the anterolateral wall of the left ventricle, the interventricular septum, and part of the anterior wall of the right ventricle. It is the most important branch of the coronary arterial tree. The circum-flex artery which courses from the left main artery along the groove between the left atrium and left ventricle, and via its branches irrigates the left atrium and the lateral and diaphragmatic walls of the left ventricle. When this artery is large (dominant artery), it also supplies part of the right ventricle.

The coronary arteries are like two trees, with trunks and large and small branches, which distribute the blood necessary for proper functioning of the heart. The left coronary artery is more important because it irrigates most of the left ventricle, which is responsible for pumping the blood into the arterial system. For this reason occlusion of the left coronary artery is incompatible with life, except in exceptionally rare cases when the right coronary artery can adequately supply the left ventricle via small vessels communicating with the left coronary arterial tree; this is known as collateral circulation.

Coronary Cineangiography

The heart, arteries, veins and the blood are "transparent" to X-rays and thus cannot be clearly seen on a radiograph. In the case of a thoracic X-ray, the space between the lungs is occupied by a white uniform image with precise borders which includes the heart and great vessels, but which does not permit visualization of any specific structure. If the bloodstream is injected with a substance which partially blocks the passage of the X-rays (called an X-ray opaque substance or contrast medium) we can see the entire cardiovascular system, outlined by the now opaque blood. If the contrast medium is injected into the cavity of the left ventricle, this chamber becomes opacified and the form and contractions of the ventricle can be studied.

In addition to the contrast medium, catheters (fine hollow tubes) are required to guide us to the injection point. The catheters are introduced into the arterial tree via the brachial artery of the arm or the femoral artery in the inguinal area, and the tip of the catheter is maneuvered to place it in the region to be examined. The contrast medium is then injected manually or by use of a specially designed power injector.

Equipment for filming the studies for documentation and analysis was developed, a task in which Mason Sones through his patience and total dedication played a leading role. Cineangiography was perfected almost exclusively in the basement of the Cleveland Clinic where Mason passed most of his life. As we shall see later, in 1958 he was the first to visualize the coronary arteries with the help of special catheters he had designed so that the catheter tip could be located directly in the origin of the artery. This was the birth of coronary cineangiography, a technique that was refined progressively and now permits us to make a detailed analysis of the distribution of the coronary circulation *in vivo* (Figure 3).

This method revolutionized our concepts about coronary arteriosclerosis. By reading the films we could precisely detect the location and distribution of the obstructions produced by the atheromatous plaques, using different filming angles to give different projections and thereby avoid errors. I have always emphasized that it is easier to perform coronary cineangiography than to read and interpret the resulting film.

Coronary cineangiography has not just permitted us to make an objective diagnosis of coronary arteriosclerosis. The analysis of thousands of films has provided us with the basis for understanding the natural history of the disease, principally thanks to the work of Dr. Bill Proudfit and his collaborators. It has also permitted us to decide on the most adequate treatment in each case and to follow up the outcome of surgical treatment with irrefutable scientific rigor, particularly in the groups of patients submitted to different techniques of myocardial revascularization.

Our knowledge of coronary arteriosclerosis can undoubtedly be divided into two periods: that before and that after coronary cineangiography, which is tantamount to

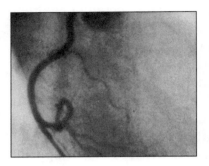

Fig. 3A. *Right coronary artery in the right anterior oblique projection.*

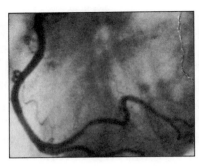

Fig. 3B. *Right coronary artery in the left anterior oblique projection.*

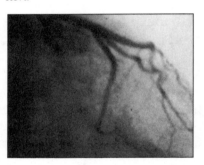

Fig. 3C. *Left coronary artery in the right anterior oblique projection.*

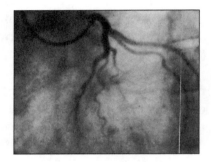

Fig. 3D. *Left coronary artery in the left anterior oblique projection.*

saying before and after Mason Sones.

With the passing of years the use of new contrast media, new catheters, and high-precision cineangiography equipment has reduced the risk of the technique to insignificance. In most cases the patient can return home the same day, and at most might be hospitalized for 24 hours. The risk is also minimal in elderly patients (over age 70) whose number has increased significantly, particularly over the past decade.

On returning to Argentina in 1971 I encountered great resistance by patients when coronary angiography was indicated (this persists even today, although less commonly). I would explain clearly the benefits we would obtain from the study, and that we were confronted by a disease which at times is unforgiving. I would inform them that 35 percent of patients suffering their first myocardial infarct never had chest pain, the infarct being the first indication of the disease, that half the patients dying from coronary arteriosclerosis died suddenly and that 40 percent of this group had no previous indication of coronary disease. Sudden death may be the first manifestation. Only in this way could the patients understand that the minimal risk of coronary cineangiography could pay big dividends.

Coronary arteriosclerosis is a treacherous disease, and we must gain the upper hand in our fight against it. I believe that you will now have no trouble in understanding the message that follows.

René G. Favaloro

Acknowledgments

First I would like to express my gratitude to Dr. Peter Willshaw, a distinguished physiologist of our Department of Basic Research, who translated the Spanish version into English; to Dr. William Proudfit, who meticulously read the manuscript several times with excellent suggestions and wrote an extremely generous foreword; finally to my good friend Ms. Rita Feran, who made the final corrections with dedication and expertise.

1

The Big Decision
The Beginnings

In a previous book I have described how in May 1950 my brother and I went to Jacinto Aráuz, a small town in the West of the Province of La Pampa, where we established ourselves as general practitioners. This move was made shortly after I graduated in medicine, having served my internship in the old Hospital Policínico of La Plata, the city of my birth. By then, I had acquired excellent training, especially in general surgery.

This "internal exile" was provoked by various motives, among which predominated my love and respect for liberty, which at that time was curtailed by the policies of the government in office. It signified an end to my first steps in thoracic surgery, which I had been following in the Rawson Hospital in Buenos Aires under the instruction of the Finochietto brothers who had developed a school of surgery which became of great importance in the training of Argentine and other Latin American surgeons. I went there every Wednesday to observe carefully the operations, especially those performed by Oscar Vaccarezza and Horacio Resano, in order to repeat them later in the Polyclinic Hospital in La

Plata. My academic activity in the department of surgery at the University of La Plata also came to an end.

We worked with dedication and effort in our rural setting, and were eventually able to transform a large old house into a 23-bed clinic with a completely equipped surgery. Our diagnostic methods even included a high-definition serial x-ray machine. Our area of practice was large, about 100 miles in all directions, and emergency cases poured in every day. With Juan José we operated on any patient who could be defined as general surgery, including obstetrics and gynecology. We occasionally operated for esophageal cancer. We attended everyone, without distinction of race, religion, politics, or ability to pay. We earned the respect of the population and lived happily. Despite all this, my soul still yearned for my old hospital and I still dreamed about thoracic surgery, which in those days was just beginning to include cardiovascular surgery. I became even more excited reading about the latest advances in the medical journals we received in Jacinto Aráuz, and remember the names of Blalock, Crafoord, Gross, Harken and Lillehei as the principal contributors. In my infrequent visits to La Plata I began to express to Professor Mainetti my desire to leave rural medicine and travel to the United States. I must confess - and I hope not to be misunderstood- that although I was filled with satisfaction at the end of every successful operation, I could not help thinking to myself "This is not the place for you, it never was; you are capable of bigger things and you are wasting your time."

In the Colegio Nacional of the University of La Plata, the secondary school attached to the University, I was always classified in the upper third of my group. The absolute leadership was disputed between ' Lungo ' Rojas with whom I went on to study medicine and 'Traga' Mattanó who later studied engineering. One day as I was walking alone through the woods, in a grove of oak trees as I vividly remember, on my way to the medical school where the course had begun a few weeks earlier, I entered into a dialogue with my own soul as I often do in these moments of meditation: "Why can't you be first ? You have all that is needed. You just require a little more force and dedication. You must do it." This was a decisive moment in my life; from then on I would always try to be first, fighting fairly and receiving as a reward only the profound spiritual enjoyment that goes with it and which nothing can replace. Perhaps the reader can now understand a little more clearly why I decided to leave Jacinto Aráuz.

Towards the end of 1961, Professor Mainetti traveled to the United States on one of his many visits to exchange ideas and, on his return, to introduce the new techniques he personally had seen and evaluated. In this way he maintained his department in the lead. On this occasion, I asked him to find out all he could about thoracic and cardiovascular surgery so that he could advise me on where to go for training in the specialty.

When he came back he told me that if I was still determined to go, the best place would be the Cleveland Clinic. This surprised me, because at that time the institution was little known in Latin America. He gave me his reasons: " My friendship with Dr. Crile has permitted me to see the work of Dr. Mason Sones and his colleagues in the catheterization labs and they are undoubtedly years ahead of any other cardiology center in the United States. If only you could see the coronary angiograms! Then there is Dr. Willem Kolff who is directing research in the Department of Artificial Organs - what they are doing is incredible! I have watched Dr. Effler very closely, and he seems to me to be an excellent surgeon. I believe it to be the ideal place for you."

Knowing him as I did - Professor Mainetti was the most brilliant surgeon you could wish to see in an operating room, and was gifted with a lucid and balanced intelligence - I happily told him that I accepted his recommendation without reservation. We agreed that he would write to Dr.

Crile immediately. Two months passed by, without receiving a reply. I decided to travel anyhow, so that I personally could acquaint myself with the work at the Cleveland Clinic and explore my possible appointment. I was still left with the task of convincing my family, especially my mother.

My father was a cabinet-maker, and in his modest workshop art tended to triumph over economics. Over the years he had developed great skill in working with wood, and was by nature creative. He would transform the planks that had slowly weathered on the empty lot next to the workshop into unique pieces of different styles to grace the homes of his clients, many of whom were from Buenos Aires. At his side I learned all the secrets, and the hours passed by unnoticed as I worked with the various types of gouges to reproduce the beauty hidden in the drawings we used as models.

Even though I helped out, especially during vacations, as just another laborer veneering or carving wood, the income from the shop was just not sufficient to support the whole family and much less if my parents aspired to a university education for their sons. As a result, my mother took on work as a dressmaker and contributed significantly to the household income, often laboring late at night after having completed all the usual domestic chores. Due to her efforts, her sons could then graduate from medical school. My parents taught me both ethics and hard work; nothing can be gained without effort. My father did not know what it was to take a rest. When the few employees had gone home at the end of the day he would continue working until it was time for the evening meal. His work continued on Saturdays and Sundays until late at night. On Sundays he would break his rhythm to knead the dough which my mother had prepared for the pasta, until his palms had left it warm to the touch.

How often I remember the image of my mother bent over the old pedal-driven Singer sewing machine with her hands transforming the colorful cloths of her moneyed clients into impeccable dresses. With pain reflected in her clear, deep and tender eyes she accepted my explanations: "If it is for your own good, son, you must do it. Let's hope that these two or three years you are talking about go flying by. You will write to me often won't you?"

Juan José continued working for a time in Aráuz before returning to La Plata with his sons to assuage our absence. I did not wish anyone to accompany us to the airport, knowing beforehand that the final moments would be heart-rending. We who have Italian blood in our veins are, fortunately, also very sensitive.

It was the first time that my wife and I had boarded an airplane, a 707 of Aerolineas Argentinas, and we were a little scared. Fortunately the flight was uneventful. Ideas were whirling in my head and I slept fitfully. Had I done right? I had cut short my career as a country doctor, which had given me so many happy moments. Without doubt we had improved medical attention for thousands of unprotected patients and we had achieved a level of economic stability, but was I sufficiently well-prepared? Would I have the aptitude to enter into the field of thoracic and cardiovascular surgery? Would I be accepted in the Cleveland Clinic? Would I be able to communicate in English? Perhaps I would be back home sooner than expected. In addition to secondary school English, for the past few months I had spent hours and hours with Mr. Leach, a private teacher of Australian origin, but I did not know for certain how much I had learned. If we were accepted, would we be capable of adapting to a society so different from our own? Without doubt, at the age of 39 I would be faced once more with a great challenge. Would it be too late? I did not think so, for the years spent without a moment's rest in Aráuz had made me strong and given me an extraordinary power of resistance.

We flew the whole night and arrived at Kennedy in the

morning. Customs and immigration were no problem thanks to our immigrant visas, a lot easier to obtain then than now. We had decided to spend the rest of the day in a hotel near the airport. Our flight to Cleveland was not due to leave until the following morning. Our first contact was with a porter who willingly helped us and indicated the most appropriate hotel. What surprised me most was the ease of communication with him. I had passed my first English test without any problem, which soothed my nerves. I was thankful to Mr. Leach. In the hotel, we rested after showering and that evening went down to the restaurant where we ate grilled chicken and ordered the famous American apple pie which had figured so many times in my English lessons. It looked very appetizing when the waiter set it before us, but on tasting it I was disillusioned to discover that it was flavored with cinnamon, which I later found to be a common ingredient in American cooking. I detest cinnamon. Even its aroma turns my stomach. I had to go without dessert in my first American meal because I did not dare even to ask for ice cream. The next day we flew to Cleveland, and once in a taxi I managed, with a certain amount of difficulty, to tell the driver that we wanted to go to the Cleveland Clinic and that we had not made reservations in any nearby hotel. He was of the opinion that as we were strangers and did not know the district it would be convenient for us to lodge in the Bolton Square Hotel which was close to the Clinic. It was an old red brick building on the corner of Carnegie and East 89th, and was modest but clean.

That same afternoon I went over to the Clinic which in those days occupied the block between Euclid and Carnegie avenues and 90th and 93rd streets (Figure 4). I entered for the first time via the main door on 93rd street. I asked for Dr. George Crile's office and once there I gave Professor Mainetti's letter of presentation to the receptionist. After a short wait, the secretary showed me in. Crile welcomed me affectionately, sat me down in front of his

Fig. 4. *The Cleveland Clinic when I arrived.*

desk, returned to reading my mentor's letter, and confessed that for various reasons had not been able to answer the two previous ones. I explained the motive for my journey and apologized for my poor English. He answered that it was by no means poor and that we would have no difficulty in communicating. To me, this seemed an excess of generosity and goodwill on his part for I was only too conscious of my shortcomings. In time I discovered that these were only two of his merits. Who would have imagined that this first meeting was just the beginning of a valuable exchange of ideas with a man of exceptional talents. In addition to his duties as a surgeon, continuing the initiative of his father, who in 1921 was one of the founders of the Cleveland Clinic, Crile is a profound humanist who is convinced by his observations, especially of animal behavior, that we can all live in peace and harmony. He is a lover of nature and of the absolute liberty of man, evidenced by his books: *A Naturalistic View of Man, The Importance of Early Training in Learning, Living and the Organization of Society*. For me it was a privilege to philosophize about important themes of modern society and to analyze their notorious faults, especially when we met with our wives to spend a weekend in his country house. Under his head of gray hair, his analytical brain absorbed, dissected, and decanted what his blue eyes had seen in nature, during his extensive travels, or in his avid reading. His unusual intelligence was notable, for example, during the monthly case discussions when he would sit at the back of the room and listen in attentive silence only to surprise us at the end of the presentation with some observation of genuine clinical value despite the fact that many of the cases presented were outside his specific field. Years later, in 1968, he surprised me yet again. At that time, renal transplants were commonly performed in the Clinic. In an attempt to improve the results, it was routine practice to remove the thymus and spleen from the potential recipient weeks or months before the main operation. The day after I had performed my first heart transplant, we were changing our clothes in the morning before beginning our work in the operating rooms. He asked me how the patient was getting along and after I had told him everything was well he asked me "Did you remove the thymus?" I stood rooted to the spot. The transplant had been performed using a frontal approach, dividing the sternum. The remains of the thymus were still there in the upper part of the incision lying in the fat which is normally associated with the pericardium covering the heart. My reply was negative, and he made no comment. I thought "once more he has shown that he does not miss a single detail." It appeared incredible to me that I had not removed the thymus, which would have taken only a few minutes (Figure 5).

After understanding the motive of my visit he phoned Dr. Donald B. Effler, Chief of the Department of Thoracic and Cardiovascular Surgery, who agreed to receive me. He took his leave of me with a "good luck young fellow" and I went in search of Dr. Effler to the ninth floor where "Desk 91" was located. At the end of a long corridor, I found Dr. Effler's office. His secretary Eleanor occupied a small room next door, and it was she who showed me in to him and made the corresponding presentation.

Effler was sitting behind his desk and on rising I could verify his great height and athletic build which showed through his short-sleeved white shirt. He had a wide face with somewhat prominent cheekbones which emphasized his inquisitive and penetrating eyes behind the bifocals.

As I had done previously with Crile, I explained the reasons for my visit and stressed my deep interest in his specialty. He asked me if I had passed the examination required for foreign medical graduates who wished to take postgraduate training in the U.S., the E.C.F.M.G. exam. After expressing my ignorance of its existence, he told me that it was an indispensable legal requirement without which no hospital could accept a resident. As a solution, he offered the possibility of my being an observer on a day-by-day basis. He made it clear that I would not receive a salary. Later on, if I was still interested, I could sit for the exam and regularize my situation. I, in turn, made it clear to him that my previous medical activities had allowed me to save some money and I was neither asking for nor expecting a salary. I only hoped that he authorize me to report to work every

George Crile, Jr.

F. Mason Sones, Jr.

William L. Proudfit

Donald B. Effler

Fig. 5

day, obeying the limits appropriate to observer status, in order to learn. I promised to work with dedication and responsibility. We agreed on these terms and he told me that I should now go to the Education Department in order to officially register my presence as an "observer."

To get there, I had to return to the central hall, then follow a long corridor to the West, and after taking an elevator make my way to the office of Dr. Leedham, "the colonel", Director of Education. On entering, my rural doctor's instinct told me that all was not well with Dr. Leedham's attitude. So it turned out to be. When I told him that I came from Argentina he immediately replied "You belong to a wild country. I don't know what sort of education you people receive. Recently, a doctor from your country signed a contract to work with Dr. Kolff on the artificial heart project and a month later disappeared without saying anything. It seems that he is now working in Houston. You should realize that in our country that counts as a serious offense. It is immoral." He continued to proffer insults to Argentina, so I instinctively rose and told him: "I am not going to tolerate one more insult to my country. We are not so savage as you imagine. You cannot judge all the university graduates of Argentina on the basis of the attitude of only one of them. I am sorry but I am going to leave."

You can imagine how I felt at this moment. I had gone to the interview full of happiness and enthusiasm as a consequence of the good treatment I had received from Crile and Effler, and in just a few minutes all had been destroyed. I could see myself beginning the return journey. I decided to go back to Effler's office, and was received by him after a considerable wait. I told him what had happened, my nervousness exacerbating my language difficulties. He listened in silence and then said, almost as an order: "Forget what has happened. Officially registered or not, you will present yourself on my service tomorrow at eight o'clock on the dot."

I went back to the hotel and told my wife all about the incident. The favorable talks with Crile and Effler restored my optimism. We would stay. About 7:30 the next morning I crossed the street, where some snowflakes were still drifting in the breeze before landing softly on the sidewalks covered with snow during the night. The city of Cleveland is on the shore of Lake Erie, one of the Great Lakes between the United States and Canada. The temperature of the water is always higher than that of the land during winter and as a result enormous cloud banks are continuously forming. The cold North wind brings snowfalls which begin in the middle of December and usually last until April. A wintry sun appears only occasionally. We did not see a single ray of sun for 28 days after our arrival. Communications remained uninterrupted because the continuous use of snow plows in the cities and on the highways clear the snow and spread salt or grit. During my entire time in the U.S., we had to stay in the Clinic only once, because a severe and unexpected snowstorm at the beginning of November prevented us from returning to our homes. In January, February and part of March the cold is very intense with temperatures dropping to 12 to 15 centigrade degrees below zero and occasionally to 18, but this is made tolerable by the use of central heating in all the buildings.

When we were preparing for our visit to the States we bought, in Argentina, woolen underwear including long underpants like our grandparents had used, thick shirts and tightly knitted, high-necked sweaters. We never used them. We found that the only clothing necessary outdoors was an overcoat; the temperature in apartments, houses and above all in the Clinic being maintained at springtime levels. We doctors, for example, used shortsleeved shirts and light slacks and of course the classic white coat.

On arriving at the Clinic, I went to the second floor to the Department of Surgery. This consisted of 18 operating rooms, the postoperative intensive care unit, the Pathology

Department, a room for extracorporeal circulation, and at the end on the left a lounge with coffee always ready, hot water for those who preferred tea, abundant milk, and cookies to replace lost calories. To one side was the room where each member of the surgical staff had a locker to change clothes, and right next door was the residents room also fitted with lockers. A small room contained the "greens", that is to say the trousers and tops of that color which residents, auxiliaries, and visitors wore to replace their street clothes or the whites used in the rest of the hospital. Uly, a man of somewhat advanced age as evidenced by his gray hair, kept everything clean and tidy in the locker rooms and the lounge. He was loved by everyone, always smiling and friendly. He spoke with an accent which took me some time to understand, but eventually we became good friends. He had taken upon himself as an obligation the task of polishing the shoes of the staff doctors and occasionally distinguished a resident by doing the same for him.

The work of the Department of Thoracic and Cardio-vascular Surgery began in the morning with the endoscopies, which were performed using local anesthesia in a specially prepared room. At that time, pulmonary and esophageal diseases were predominant. Dr. Effler presented me to his associate, Dr. Larry Groves, to the chief resident Dr. Niall Scully, to the junior resident Dr. Alfonso Parisi, and to the general surgical resident who was rotating through Thoracic Surgery as part of his training. This was the entire medical group.

The endoscopies were performed with great rapidity, Effler and Groves having accumulated a vast experience in this procedure. With the passing of time, I was impressed by the diagnostic precision of the cytological studies under the charge of J.B. Hazard, chief of the Department of Pathology, who would present the results in only a few minutes. Once the endoscopies were finished, the group went to rooms 17 and 18 to begin the surgical work. As I have already mentioned, there were many pulmonary resections and a great deal of esophageal disease. Effler was an expert in both, and had developed personal techniques for the repair of hiatus hernias and the correction of megaesophagus. In addition, operations were performed for ductus, coarctation, and palliative surgery principally using the techniques of Blalock or Potts in the cyanotic patients, usually very young children.

Surgery using extracorporeal circulation was performed on Tuesdays, Wednesdays and Fridays on one patient per day, the great majority being congenital defects. In these cases the patient is connected to a device which oxygenates and pumps the blood, temporarily replacing the functions of the heart and lungs. This is why it is commonly called the heart-lung machine.

Extracorporeal circulation was first used by Gibbon in 1953 and still represented a real challenge because it provoked changes in the patient's own blood as well as requiring large quantities of donors blood to fill the dead space of the oxygenator and tubing of the heart-lung machine.

Those first days gave me a global idea of the complexity of the work being carried out in the Clinic and of the enormous responsibility which I would have to confront if I wished to qualify in this specialty. As may be imagined, no one really noticed me and I confess that I exchanged only a few words, particularly with the nurses and auxiliaries. Every afternoon I went back to the hotel and shared my impressions with my wife, analyzing what I had observed.

One of our first tasks was to look for a bank to deposit the money we had brought with us and which represented all our capital. Just a few blocks from the clinic was a branch of one of the most solid banks of Cleveland. Dr. Effler advised me to go there and open an account which he told me was a simple thing to do. Indeed it was. We spoke to the first unoccupied clerk we saw who introduced us to a more important employee, who had his own desk, and who asked us what we needed. He filled a card with our personal details including passport and immigrant visa numbers, registered our signatures, and in a few minutes gave us a small book in which our deposit of something over 10 thousand dollars had been credited. This book was to be presented every time we wished to deposit or withdraw money, and was accompanied by a check book with our names imprinted. He advised us to use it for most of our expenses, even the smallest ones, because that is how things were done in the United States. We were amazed that all the paperwork had been done by only one employee! We were accustomed to the bureaucracy of our country and just could not understand the simplicity of this first contact. Further visits to the bank confirmed our first impression. When we needed money, we presented the check and the little book at the teller's window, he registered the check number, subtracted the quantity, and noted the balance with a simple pen (computers did not exist then). The balance was then noted on the card held by the bank.

We had to be very careful of our expenditures because we did not know how long it would take me to prepare for and pass the exam, or if I would then be accepted as a "Fellow" of the clinic. To reduce costs we moved to a hotel on the North side of Euclid and East 96th, which rented rooms with kitchenette and refrigerator. Although these facilities were minimal, my wife could now cook thus eliminating restaurant bills. A few yards from the hotel were two supermarkets, Abood's Food and Pick and Pay, which were of modest size but offered everything, in particular Abood's. We began to discover the excellence of the goods and the labor-saving benefits for the housewife. For example, soups were available in cans. They were delicious and only required heating. I was particularly fond of Campbell's cream of mushroom and cream of pea. They cost about seven to ten cents a can, and if a little cooked rice was added to them they made a complete meal. We were surprised at the price of chicken, about one third the price of beef, exactly the opposite being the case in Argentina. My wife frequently prepared chicken in the oven or in the saucepan with onion, tomato, and peppers which we ate with different types of pasta. What was really surprising in the middle of winter was the quality, cleanliness, and availability of a variety of fruits and vegetables which came from the South. Despite having been transported for hundreds of miles, they appeared to be recently harvested. The secret was the use of refrigerated transport to maintain freshness and later storage in specially-built bins. The shelves were replenished several times a day as needed. Storerooms with controlled temperature and humidity were not only to be seen in the big supermarkets, but also in virtually any shop selling fruits and vegetables. This would appear to be an expensive extra, but consideration of the losses caused by inadequate storage especially during summer when fruit deteriorates rapidly and must be discarded reveals that the benefits outweigh the costs.

Even today during my frequent visits to La Plata I see how the produce of the small growers around my native city are transported to Buenos Aires in open trucks exposed to the inclemencies of the weather especially during summer, and even in the Capital the goods are on open-air display in the fruit and vegetable shops. How much we still have to learn. After a few weeks, we realized that our food costs would be considerably less than we had thought.

The old hotel was the residence of many elderly persons. Every night they would get together in the central lobby and chat among themselves or watch television on the only set available. In time, we too came to occupy a place in these meetings and were the object of much interest for having in some way broken the monotony. We were surprised to find out that the majority of these old folks had families, in some cases quite numerous, who would visit with them on weekends and take them out for a few hours. This appeared horrific to us. How was it possible that such a developed society had reached this extreme? That grandparents were regarded as a nuisance to the rest of the family seemed like heresy to us. In a few cases this might have been justifiable, but in general we were saddened, especially by those who suffered a certain degree of mental confusion. With the passing of the years something similar but to a much lesser degree is happening today in Argentina. There is no doubt that life expectancy has increased in proportion to advances in medicine and that the geriatric population represents a steadily growing socioeconomic problem. A suitable solution must be found, but these people should not be thrown into poorly furnished hotels or stacked like logs in old people's homes, unprotected and badly cared for.

I continued to arrive punctually at the Hospital, and during the afternoons I would fill notebooks with my observations, particularly the details of the surgical techniques. My contacts with the different members of the group steadily increased. Scully, the Chief Resident, was a mature surgeon who had worked for a number of years in his native Hawaii and was now completing his training so that he could take the Board Certification examination which if he passed would permit him to exercise the profession of thoracic and cardiovascular surgeon.

To obtain this qualification, the medical graduate must work as a rotating intern for one year, then work four years in general surgery after which he can take the corresponding Board examination, and finally two years in his elected specialty. The certifications and examinations are controlled by the medical colleges, in our case by the American Association for Thoracic Surgery; the programs leave no chance for the use of influence or personal recommendation.

Scully had decided to specialize in thoracic surgery, choosing Cleveland as his place of study. He had a good surgical touch and his experience was obvious in the operating field. Perhaps because we were the same age and both had practiced general surgery for years, our relationship progressed rapidly. In just a few weeks we got to know each other well and in the final months before his departure I was his required assistant every time Effler assigned him an operation.

Alfonso Parisi - Al to everyone - was Canadian. His father was a Sicilian who had "discovered America" in Hamilton, Ontario, starting as a street seller. It is interesting that the Italian immigrants of the last century and the beginning of this century settled in the northeast of the United States and to a lesser extent in Canada. How is it that coming from a sunny country they decided on a region which is extremely cold and covered with snow for months each year? The reason is simple. In the South, there were many black people working in agriculture that fitted the socioeconomics of rural production. Blacks rarely lived in the northeast during those years, and the Italians supplanted them in all the "dirty" jobs. The early years were extremely hard, and it would take time to relate all the difficulties they had to face and which I got to know from the older Italians and their descendants. We had something important in common with Parisi: the Favaloros were also Sicilian. This similar origin which could be seen in our darker skin, more obvious in my own case, drew us together in our daily tasks and we soon became friends. He helped me in everything, and was like a brother to me who despite being younger guided my early progress and was always prepared to respond to my innumerable anxieties. From his position as Chief Resident following Scully, his sound advice was definitive in getting me settled in the Department of Thoracic and Cardiovascular Surgery.

Dr. Larry Groves, a Harvard graduate, was an eminent surgeon. He made even the most difficult maneuvers appear easy thanks to his being ambidextrous. It was a real pleasure to watch him operate on small children, sometimes newborns, correcting congenital cardiac defects incompatible with life or an esophago-tracheal fistula. He helped Effler in all the surgeries requiring extracorporeal circulation and was the only one permitted to dissect the femoral artery which in those days was used for the arterial inlet. His main defect was his lack of communication, and he would remain silent even during the afternoon rounds when the whole team visited the patients. It was obvious that his relationship with Effler did not go beyond the strictly medical. In reality, he spoke very little and when he did, his English was difficult to understand being devoid of emphasis. The Americans call this "mumbling." During the first months in which I assisted him in operations, I did so more through my surgeon's intuition than in response to his verbal requests. I once told Effler of my difficulties in understanding what Groves was saying, to which he replied "Don't worry René , I don't understand him either!" In addition to being a surgeon, Larry Groves was an expert cabinet-maker, as evidenced by the workshop in the basement of his home and the impeccable furniture in the other rooms.

The team was completed by Rose Litturi, who was in charge of the extracorporeal circulation system. She reported directly to Dr. Kolff, who had designed the enormous machine based on a Kay Cross disc oxygenator with a number of additions, including electronic flowmeters to achieve greater precision. Rose was also of Sicilian descent, evidenced by her raven hair and dark eyes. She skillfully selected her perfumes, which were all French. I have never met another perfusionist quite like her. When the patient entered into extracorporeal circulation she limited her world to the pump which she scanned ceaselessly. She could and indeed was required to interchange opinions with the rest of the team, but she did this without glancing away for a single second from the complex machine in her charge. For some months part of my work was to help her.

Fred Brown was a black man who formed part of Kolff's group and collaborated with Rose. He was very intelligent and was extremely knowledgeable in physiology. He did not just collaborate with Rose but also participated in the complex activities of Kolff's Department of Artificial Organs. Fred's wife was angelic; they were devout Catholics and had two children. He was a jovial man, always smiling and cheerful despite the economic hardships he had to suffer due to the continuation of his studies. In time, he obtained a scholarship, completed his Ph.D. and dedicated himself to teaching at Case Western Reserve University. We were great friends, and the color of his skin was of no importance. Everyone appreciated him and he was always present at the social gatherings outside the hospital organized by one or other of the members of the team. All of this served to show me that racial problems, especially those of the black population in the United States, can only be solved by education. An educated black is just like any other citizen, and education can break down the barriers of false aristocracy raised and maintained by some whites in order to defend their privileges.

The Department of Anesthesia was run by Dr. Donald E. Hale, but most of the procedures were done by special university-qualified nurses. An outstanding member of this group was Del Portzer, a mature lady with a fragile figure - I don't think she could have weighed more than 50 kilos - but with an enormous capacity for hard work and shouldering of responsibility. She had married late and unfortunately her marriage was short-lasting due to the unexpected death of her husband who suffered a heart attack in his own home. Poor Del tried to resuscitate him, but without success. From then on, she lived for her patients; not only did she monitor them moment by moment in the operating room, watching all the surgical maneuvers from the head of the table, but also followed them in the Intensive Care Unit for the first few hours until they had been stabilized and extubated. In time she became one of my essential collaborators and was present at every one of the operations which were to leave their mark on the development of cardiovascular surgery.

This group of colleagues was completed by the scrub nurses, of whom I remember Zenita, Martha, Mary, and Diane as being outstanding, and by the nurses of the intensive care unit including the unforgettable Jenny Mayer.

Effler had undoubtedly been born to be a leader as well as an eminent surgeon. He had formed a family rather than a team and this was obvious in the devotion they all had for him. The organization and planning of the different areas was notable. Effler was actively accompanied by Kolff and by Mason Sones who was head of the Department of Cardiac Catheterization. Faced with complex cases, it was common to see the three of them exchanging opinions in the operative room, often hotly in the case of Effler and Sones. To be present at such a moment was one of the greatest privileges I enjoyed in the first few months of my work. It can never be repeated. To demonstrate my gratitude, I did any job that came my way, fetching the patients and placing them on the operating table, inserting the Foley catheter to measure the quantity of urine produced during the operation, washing the skin of the thorax with the special soap routinely used in those years, connecting the drain tubes to the receptacles hung from the patient trolleys, and helping Rose to assemble and disassemble the extracorporeal circulation pump. In summary, I had converted myself from a surgeon who had performed hundreds of operations into a more or less qualified nurse, the last scraping at the bottom of the barrel. This was of no importance to me, for I realized that to get to the top it was necessary to start from the bottom. After a few weeks Effler invited me ("would you like to scrub up and help me?") to assist him in the resection of the left lung of a cancer patient. You can imagine what this meant to me. The operation was uneventful. As the second assistant I stood next to Effler, with Scully standing opposite as the first assistant. I will always remember the first question of the long series which was to follow. While dissecting the inferior pulmonary vein he asked me if I recognized this vascular structure " a fine thing it would be if I didn't," was my thought at the time. Its size and location make it easy to recognize. From that day onwards I participated in more and more operations, my poor English being subservient to my surgical skills developed over the past years.

There is a notable difference between a thoracic surgeon who deals with the lungs, esophagus, and mediastinal tumors and the surgeon who also performs cardiovascular surgery. The cardiovascular surgeon has the enormous advantage that his training gives him in approaching thoracic surgery from a unique perspective. For example, when a pulmonary tumor is near the pulmonary hilum (root) or if there is an anterior mediastinal tumor he does not hesitate to open the pericardium to gain better access to the vascular structures. He rarely uses his fingers to separate the anatomical planes, scissors being his best friend. Effler was a clear example of this difference.

It is difficult to explain quite why, but Effler and I soon established an almost affectionate relationship. We understood each other very well: I thought back to our first interview and remembered the expression on his face when I told him that I had not come to look for financial rewards, but only to learn from him. He could not hide a look which was a mixture of surprise and a certain degree of admiration. Years later he told me that my reply had caused quite an impact.

When he found that we were living in a single room with kitchenette, and faced with my insistence on living as close as possible to the clinic despite his advice to move to the Heights where most of the Fellows lived, he made all the necessary arrangements for us to get an apartment in an old building facing 90th Street and owned by the Clinic. Its name, Palais Royal, led one to believe that it must have been quite important many years ago in this part of town. It was the only one left on the block, which the Clinic had converted into a parking lot. Outside, it was a somber building whose blackened walls barely revealed the brickwork, but the apartment was fully furnished, comfortable and quite sufficient for two persons. The living-dining room was ample, there was a main bedroom and a smaller room which I used as my study, a bathroom, and a kitchen. We were surprised to discover that the apartment opposite ours was that of a doctor from Argentina, Dr. Martín Atdjian, who was a Fellow in the Rheumatology Department. It is always gratifying to discover a compatriot in a strange land. Martín helped us enormously in those early days and introduced us to other Argentine doctors doing postgraduate training. Thanks to Martín my wife got in touch with the Council of World Affairs, an organization that helps immigrants of many origins, especially in learning English. As a result, Toni attended daily classes and began to make friends with doctors' wives of many different nationalities. The Clinic itself had an organization formed by the American doctors' wives that helped orient the foreign wives in the community.

About two months after our arrival, Effler invited us to a "party" - which I later discovered in America could mean anything from a cocktail to a dinner or even a lunch - at his home in Shaker Heights, one of the most elegant suburbs to the southeast of the city. My English played a trick on me, for when we got out of the taxi on Saturday at six in the afternoon and presented ourselves on Effler's doorstep, we discovered that the party was to be the following week! I felt so ashamed and did not know how to excuse myself, but Effler showed us in while laughing all the time. After a few minutes his wife, Joanna, came downstairs and we were presented. She was in the middle of dressing for a dinner engagement at the home of some of their friends. Despite our wishing to return immediately to our apartment, they insisted on us sitting down in their spacious living room. We were so embarrassed that we could barely articulate a few phrases. Effler prepared drinks at the bar which is a feature of many American homes above a certain social standing, while Joanna chatted to ease the tension. The majority of her questions were about our homeland of which she knew nothing. She was extremely kind. Effler disappeared for a short while and returned to tell us that he had made a reservation in an Italian restaurant which they visited quite frequently, and that a taxi was on its way to pick us up. They would still be expecting us the following week! This was the unusual way in which we got to know Effler's wife and home. The taxi arrived a few minutes later and took us to Guarinos, a restaurant located in Little Italy, which is the area near Case Western Reserve University where thousands of Italians live.

True to its name, the restaurant was indeed owned by the Guarino family who were Sicilians who had emigrated after the First World War. It was famous for its pastas which were made by the family. For reasons to be explained later, we became their friends. Our first true meal in an American restaurant was delicious, more so for the bread which was just like that we ate back home in Argentina. When we asked for the check, they explained that Effler had ordered it to be put on his personal account.

The following Monday, before beginning the day's work, I once more asked Effler to excuse our error and thanked him from my heart for his hospitality. Little by little, almost without noticing it, my relationship with Effler deepened. For example, there came a time when he insisted that we use one of his cars during weekends. In general, middle class American families possess more than one car. The majority have one each for husband and wife and buy used cars for those children who have reached driving age and passed the driving test. I thanked him again and explained that we were planning to buy a car for ourselves. He had told us that used cars were available quite cheaply, but that they should be carefully selected so that an apparent bargain does not turn into a constant expense due to repair bills. He called one of his patients, owner of a Ford agency, so that we would not be cheated. We went to the agency one Saturday morning, and the owner himself showed us to the used car lot which surrounded the building and which was full of vehicles for sale. He went directly to a red Valiant and said "This is the car for you. It might cost you a little more, but is almost new. I know the owner. He changed cars without much reason, because as you can see this has only 13 thousand miles recorded and believe me, this is genuine."

I accepted his advice, despite disliking the color. I later got used to it. We went back to his office and he told us the price was $1,100, a third of the price of a new vehicle with the same features. We agreed on this price and I got out my checkbook to write a check for this amount. He stopped me, saying "What are you doing? You must finance this purchase instead of paying cash. That is how we do things here. By paying monthly installments, your bank will classify you as a good payer and then make you a loan if you need one in the future."

I thus bought a car and learned my first lesson about American economics at the same time. Almost everything was bought like that, even houses. On long-term credit, payable in installments, and at low interest thanks to the economic stability and absence of inflation during those years. How different from my own country! While I was getting my driving license, the agency owner promised to check out the Valiant carefully even though it was almost new.

To obtain my license, I had to complete a written examination and answer an endless series of questions to show that I knew the traffic rules and then go out driving with a state employee who observed, without speaking, how I drove including as the final test parking in a small space. One week later we were mobile. The Valiant lasted us three years more and it really was as though we had bought a new automobile.

I arrived at the Cleveland Clinic shortly after two important events. At the beginning of January 1962, Effler and his colleagues had successfully repaired the most important lesion of the coronary tree, severe obstruction of the main trunk of the left coronary artery, by use of a patch made from pericardium. It is well known that the heart receives its nutritive blood supply via the right and left coronary arteries. This latter is the most important because it supplies the muscular mass of the left ventricle which is responsible for pumping the blood out into the aorta and hence to the entire body. Obstruction of the left coronary artery at its origin is incompatible with life in most patients. Using extracorporeal circulation, Effler had been able to make a longitudinal incision at the site of obstruction and then had carefully sewn the small patch of pericardium over the incision. The caliber of the artery at this site had thus been augmented allowing blood flow to be reestablished.

In the second event, a few days later, Sones had performed a selective catheterization study of a patient operated on by Vineberg in Canada some years before. He demonstrated for the first time that the internal mammary artery, which had been implanted in a tunnel made in the muscle of the left ventricle, was connected by many small arteries to branches of the left coronary artery, especially the left anterior descending artery. Fresh arterial blood was thus supplied to the heart muscle despite the much reduced flow through the severely arteriosclerotic coronaries.

Arthur Vineberg had begun his experimental work in Montreal in 1946. He had standardized a model in which small rings - ameroids - were placed around the most important coronary vessels in dog hearts and in a few weeks expanded sufficiently to constrict the diameter of these vessels, thus reproducing the principal effect of coronary arteriosclerosis in humans. The next step was to dissect the internal mammary artery from the thoracic wall and to implant it into a small tunnel made in the anterolateral wall of the left ventricle, the idea being that a systemic high-flow and high-pressure artery would develop collaterals (small arteries originating from the systemic artery) connecting it to the low-pressure low-flow coronary arteries. The experimental studies confirmed this hypothesis, and Vineberg applied the implantation technique to patients selected only on clinical signs. These patients were then evaluated during followup only by recording the improvement in their clinical status. It is clearly seen that an objective evaluation was missing, and for this reason Vineberg found it difficult to convince his colleagues of the beneficial results of his technique. These colleagues had been exposed to all sorts of operations since the first attempts of Jonnesco in 1916, and were totally skeptical.

Sones was thus able to provide the first objective proof "in vivo" of the correctness of Vineberg's hypothesis. This first result was confirmed in March on a second patient, operated on by Bigelow in Toronto. As a consequence the Vineberg approach began to be used, with caution, in the Department of Thoracic and Cardiovascular Surgery.

Sones and his colleagues worked in B10, the Department of Cardiac Catheterization, located in the basement. I discovered B10 as a result of examining the cineangiographic films of the patients who had been classified as suitable for surgery. I was soon very impressed by the exceptional quality of the studies. Sones had developed cineangiography, starting off by studying congenital malformations and valvular disease. One day the catheter for injection of the contrast medium inadvertently slipped into the upper third of the right coronary artery. The contrast material destined to mix with blood and flow through the heart and great vessels suddenly filled the whole of the right coronary tree. Sones jumped to look for a scalpel to open the thorax and begin cardiac massage - at that time external massage was not yet in use - in response to what he thought would be certain cardiac paralysis. Nothing happened. The heart continued to beat and the patient did not feel a thing. For any other specialist, this would have been passed off as an unfortunate accident which luckily was without consequences, but the genius of Sones transformed the accident into the birth of selective coronary cineangiography. This happened in 1958.

The surgical activities finished in the early afternoon, and as I was only an observer I did not have any fixed duties to attend to. I did of course follow the postoperative recovery of the patients very closely, in the Intensive Care Unit and also occasionally accompanied Parisi on his rounds.

Little by little I began to visit B10 assiduously. Here I found the archives containing the case histories with detailed descriptions of the angiographic findings, photographic reproductions, and the films themselves. Without bothering anyone, I quietly analyzed every case. If I had any doubts, I would ask the Residents to help me. Now and again I would watch Sones or his associate Shirey perform a study. Mason Sones was almost always accompanied by the many visitors who came to see his work. He always wore a short-sleeved white undershirt, over which he hung the apron to protect himself from the radiation produced by the equipment, and finally the sterile gown and gloves. In addition to the few instruments necessary for the performance of the study I had noticed in the tray a long forceps, also sterile, placed so that its end jutted out over the edge of the tray some ten centimeters. Thanks to this arrangement Sones, who was an inveterate smoker, could carry on smoking while working. He would pick up a cigarette with the forceps, someone would light it for him, generally one of the nurses, and after taking a few puffs return the forceps to the tray always with the last ten centimeters, now no longer sterile, overhanging. He had acquired an exceptional ability in the identification of each coronary artery in addition to having developed the technique of cineangiography into a fine art which allowed him to obtain films of quite extraordinary definition.

On occasion, it was difficult even for the residents who had been in B10 for a long time to interpret certain films. With the help of Elaine, his secretary who combined singular beauty with an affable personality, I found myself face to face with Sones for the first time. I had brought with me two studies . He invited me to sit down, I explained what I was doing, and he immediately responded to my questions while observing the films on the Tagarno viewer reserved for his own use. This did not signify any preferential treatment. He was always disposed to share his knowledge and experience with anyone who came to his office. This was the beginning of a relationship which deepened with time until we were like brothers engaged in a common task in which the only privileges were granted to the patient who was the focal point of our activities.

In the middle of winter, living opposite the clinic had its advantages. While the majority were making their way home through streets covered with snow, I could remain long hours in B10, usually until late into the evening, analyzing dozens and dozens of coronary cineangiograms. After a few months it was clear that their interpretation demanded time, because it was rare to find two patients alike. However, it was possible to distinguish two main groups; those with well-defined lesions in the proximal segments and those who on the contrary had diffuse lesions compromising almost the entire coronary circulation.

In addition to spending time in B10, I would go to the library located in the Education Building where I could consult the journals and books important to our specialty. There I met Rita Feran who was in charge and who helped me to familiarize myself with all of the existing material. It is thanks to her that I learned how to explore each theme to its utmost limit. This was long before the introduction of modern search technologies. With the perfectly classified set of "reprints" I was able to keep myself up to date with all the diseases related to our daily tasks.

It was true that I was occasionally overwhelmed by nostalgia despite the constant flow of letters between us and Argentina. I had left untied too many loose ends in my recent past and all transplants have their difficulties, especially when the country elected is so different. In general the balance was positive. Little by little I had integrated myself into the life of the Clinic and despite being an "observer" unrecognized by the Education Department, I was no longer a stranger. I participated in operations with increasing frequency, my English was improving which helped my relationship with the various divisions, and my knowledge of the specialty was progressing at a satisfying rate.

Our small social circle was gradually expanding. Al invited us to eat at his home, and there we got to know his wife and three children. His home was just like ours, for his wife was the only daughter of a Sicilian family and took care of everything herself. She washed, cooked, ironed, and even sewed the family clothes just as my mother had done. From the first moment, Toni and Adeline became friends and shared everything. Another one, Vicente Profeta, worked as an electrician in the Maintenance Department of the Clinic. He had emigrated from Italy to Argentina where he met and married María. They then decided to tempt fortune in the United States in search of new horizons. His job was to arrive at 6 a.m. each day to check out the electrical installation of the operating rooms so that nothing would interfere with the surgeons' task. Thanks to him we met several Argentines living in Cleveland, practically all were working class families engaged in a variety of jobs. Vicente lived about 20 minutes from the Clinic. He owned his house, constructed on a spacious lot and surrounded by a variety of fruit trees. In the basement, an important place in Cleveland homes due to the long cold winters, and which was in reality more like another floor of the house rather than just a cellar, he had installed a small kitchen and living room. We would meet there with other Argentine families, usually on Saturdays, everyone bringing a contribution to the meal (to Vicente's annoyance) and play one of our traditional card games called truco, which reminded us of our beloved country.

On May 25, which is the national day of Argentina, about 40 families would meet in a sports club which had a soccer field where before savoring the Argentine-style barbecue, named asado, we would play the traditional soccer match between bachelors and married men, which was not complete without the "Argentine touch." To increase the emotional content of the game, each member of the winning team would receive a cup. These cups were like those presented in important national or international matches but much smaller. They had been donated, I do not remember by whom. It was reasonable to think that the bachelors would win the match because they were younger and had more chance to practice, but midway through the second half the married men were winning two to one. At the end of the regulation 90 minutes the result was the same and the referee, who was also the father of one of the bachelors, allowed the game to go on despite our repeated protests until the other side scored a goal and the match was a draw. We had played no less than 20 minutes extra. The discussion which followed seemed endless, occasioned largely by the trophies. We finally decided to play an additional 15 minutes. When this time was almost up we had the opportunity of a free kick in the style of a short corner shot, thanks to an infraction over a sideline. I asked to take the shot, and decided to kick the ball violently towards the goal area without letting it rise into the air, in the hope that any rebound would benefit us. The ball hit a bachelor, and one of our team then kicked it gently into goal. We thus won the cups much to the displeasure of the referee.

What I remember best about these spring days is standing in the sunlight singing our national anthem which few of us could finish because we always ended in tears holding hands or embracing each other and thinking of our distant land.

With the help of Martín Atdjian we discovered the large market in the city center, just like the ferias back home, with innumerable stalls where we could buy vegetables, fresh fruits, eggs, cold meats, cheese, and best quality beef, all much cheaper than in an ordinary American supermarket. We would to go there on Saturdays and despite it being a roofed market occupying almost an entire city block I felt as though I were walking around one of the street markets so typical of my native city.

There, we got to know Jack and Mary Forestiere who were the owners of a fruit and vegetable stall that they ran with meticulous attention. The majority of their clients were black people who came to buy "greens," a wide variety of vegetables that they consumed in abundance. Jack and Mary treated everyone equally, and had the unusual custom of conversing with every customer, especially Mary who seemed to know the great majority by their first names. We gradually got to know them better, and they discovered our nationality from our accent and learned of my work in the Clinic. Thereafter, part of the conversation was always conducted in Italian, because, believe it or not, they too were of Sicilian origin!

After a while, they invited us to their home and we established a friendship which has lasted over the years. Every time we go to Cleveland it is a must for us to visit with them in their home now located in Independence.

Jack and Mary were friends of the Guarinos and so we would occasionally lunch with them on Sundays at the same restaurant we had known through Effler. The Guarinos gradually became intimate friends, so much so, that we were godparents at the first communion of one of their grandchildren.

Thanks to our automobile we widened our knowledge of the region and with the coming of spring we would escape from the city, preferably to the west, along the highway between Cleveland and Sandusky. This was a farming area mainly dedicated to the production of fruits and vegetables. The farmers would leave their produce on sale at the side of the road together with a price list and a sort of cash box or at times a simple bottle because they were generally busy with their usual tasks on the farm. Customers would select what they wanted and leave payment in the cash box or bottle. This surprised us because all depended on the good faith of the customer. I am certain that somebody at sometime went away without paying, but on our frequent trips to this area while we were living in Cleveland we saw the same system in use every summer, which testified that decency had prevailed.

The most extraordinary example was the farmer who produced nothing else but eggs. He had transformed one room of his house into an egg store kept at constant temperature. He was not there most Sundays, but we would just walk in and select our eggs. Normally we would leave a dollar, which was the stipulated price, in the cash box hung on the wall and walk out with three dozen eggs.

The most appetizing of all the fruits were the peaches. It is well known that this type of fruit needs cold winters to produce good crops, and this condition was met in Cleveland. The peaches from medium sized trees were simply exquisite. A farmer, with whom we made friends through our common love of the soil above all other things, taught us how to cook sweetcorn in the husk over a slow fire, turning it over now and again. After a half hour the husk had only barely changed color, and on removing it appeared the corn on the cob which had lost none of its flavor as it does when boiled.

Near Sandusky there was a beautiful forested public park provided with cement fireplaces for cooking and tables with benches. It was a place to take the family and cook hamburgers or hot-dogs. The ample fireplaces allowed two or three families to share the same fire. In time we got to know various parks like this near Cleveland and enjoyed visiting them and communing with nature. The most noteworthy for us was to see how, at the end of the day, the park was just as neat and tidy as when we arrived. Not a single piece of paper was left on the grass. It was a frequent sight to see how parents and grandparents went around picking up what the children had thrown on the ground and disposing of it in the trash cans dispersed among the trees. The public bathrooms were spotless, and provided with plenty of soap and toilet tissue. I thought of my own country and the deplorable state of the public parks and squares at the end of every Sunday.

A stretch of the road to Sandusky runs along the shore of Lake Erie, and about 40 miles from Cleveland there was a wooden jetty where a few fishermen would try their luck. We decided to buy some light fishing gear, both of us being lovers of this sport, and to join the rest of the fishermen now and again on Sunday afternoons. With the arrival of the warmer weather the temperature of the lake would begin to rise and the fish were more active. We soon realized that everyone hoped to catch perch of about a pound in weight. This proved to be a worthy pursuit as we found out for ourselves on cooking our own catch. Once in a while we would haul out a fish similar to our own hake or white bass, some of them weighing up to five pounds. It was entertaining to play them with only lightweight fishing gear, but we noted that many fishermen would return them to the lake or give them away, asserting that they were not of good quality. I could not believe this, but at the Clinic I was assured it was true. One day I decided to keep one because on inspecting it I was convinced that its flesh would be flavorsome if cooked properly and indeed it was. One Sunday these fish abounded in the lake and I took four of the biggest home with me. We invited Scully and Parisi and their wives to join us for a "fish dinner" in our apartment. We cooked the fish according to an old family recipe. Two centimeter thick slices of potato were carefully arranged at the bottom of the roasting tray. The bellies of the fish were filled with onion, capsicum peppers and tomatoes, and more of this was used to cover the fish, and the dressing finished with a little oil, salt, pepper and ground chili. After eating a shrimp starter, we served our fish which was thoroughly enjoyed by our guests. At the end of the meal, while having coffee, we revealed the truth about the main dish and they all expressed surprise. Goodness knows what was the origin of the legend about those "unsavory" fish whose name I don't even remember now.

　　Unfortunately, the part of Lake Erie near the city was heavily contaminated and from time to time hundreds of dead fish would float to the surface. Contamination from industrial effluents was affecting nearly all the lakes and rivers of the United States. Few precautions had been taken and to alter the situation would demand time and money which not everyone was disposed to pay. From what I could see during a visit to Cleveland at the end of '91 the situation is much the same as before. A TV program showed that in the region of the Great Lakes contamination has produced significant mutations in fish and birds. This is one of the most urgent themes of the present day. If we do not recognize the ecological disaster unleashed by man all over the planet, Argentina being no exception, the consequences will be terrible. The World Wildlife Foundation has estimated that by the year 2050 half the varieties of plants, animals and insects could disappear. This does not sound so bizarre if we consider 1) erosion of the ozone layer due to the use of chemicals, particularly those containing chlorofluorocarbons; 2) contamination of the air, principally by industrial plants, leading to acid rain that caused so much damage to forests and lakes; 3) contamination of rivers and even seas through years of dumping industrial waste and pesticides; 4) burial of hazardous wastes that pollute underground water; 5) the elimination of tropical forests, particularly in the Amazon basin; 6) diminishing supplies of potable water; 7) impoverishment of soil by overuse of farmland (this can be seen in certain parts of the pampas) and 8) diminishing fish stocks through over fishing. We must all take part in the fight to rehabilitate the air, water and land. Education about the dangers of contamination must be mandatory, starting at primary school level.

What I did not neglect, and Effler would now and then ask me about it, was my preparation for the exam. I had to return to studying, after so many years, the basic medical sciences for a large proportion of the questions referred to physiology, biochemistry, and anatomy. In addition to learning about some diseases peculiar to the United States I had also to review clinical medicine, general surgery, obstetrics and gynecology, pediatrics, and hygiene.

Apart from doing a little shopping, I spent Saturdays studying and studying in my small office until late at night only to begin again on Sunday mornings. It was like returning to my student days. I must admit that I found some of the themes to be boring, but I was obliged to pass the exam if I wished to continue in my specialty and so worked with dedication, glued to my chair.

Once in a while I would evaluate my progress using the little books for that purpose, which in addition to giving me an idea of how I was progressing, also served as valuable training for the exam, there being only about one minute available for answering each question. The exam could be taken on two occasions each year and the next date available was in September.

At the beginning of June, Effler called me from his office and told me that every year he took vacation on an island in Canada which had belonged to Dr. Higgins, emeritus surgeon in the Department of Urology. Effler enjoyed hunting and fishing and years later we went out together a few times to practice these sports. This year he had a problem because Gretchen, his daughter, had to take a few exams and would not be able to travel with them to the island. He proposed that Toni and I move into his house in Shaker Heights and live with his daughter, who was only 17 at that time.

We had gotten to know Gretchen on our visits to Effler's home. She was an enchantingly and freshly beautiful girl, full of sweetness and affection. I told him that I would consult with Toni but of course thought that it would be perfectly all right. When I discussed the idea with my wife, she was somewhat reluctant because of the tremendous responsibility of looking after an adolescent in a country where so much freedom was given to the young. I did not know how to tell this to Effler, who had shown so much confidence in us. I finally was frank with him and said what Toni thought. He told me "Don't worry René, Joanna will talk to Toni." And that is what happened. Joanna called Toni and explained that Gretchen, like most young people in this country, knew her rights and obligations and was authorized to go out with her friends and return home at any hour she chose. Toni was not to worry, because Gretchen was mature for her age and we would not have any problems. Reassured by these explanations, we moved into Effler's house for three weeks. In less than two days, Gretchen had us eating out of the palm of her hand. Toni was happy with her company and cooked typical Argentine meals that Gretchen devoured, enthusing over our simple milanesas (thin slices of steak breaded and fried), tortillas, and sausages similar to those we call chorizos that we had discovered in Alesci's and Imported Foods, two typical Italian shops, or recently baked bread that I bought in an Italian bakery on 322nd on my way back from the Clinic. Gretchen had her "boy friend" with whom she would go out, returning late at night especially on weekends. I confess that I lay awake until she was safely in her room.

The house itself was surrounded by gardens, and on seeing some empty spaces to the rear I bought a few tomato and pepper plants and planted them carefully in the most sunlit spots. On her return from vacation I explained to Joanna what I had done to her garden, and from the expression on her face it was clear that she did not approve. I asked her to let the plants grow, that the peppers did not require any special attention, and that I would tend the tomatoes, buying the stakes necessary to support them as they grew. The soil was extremely fertile and at the beginning of September Joanna called to tell me with great happiness that she had just tried the first tomatoes and found them to be delicious. From then on, every summer she continued to cultivate a few vegetables and she agreed that they were a beautiful addition to the flowers.

Effler's family group was completed by two sons, and was a typical example of a middle class family of the time. The outstanding characteristic was that the sons were taught from an early age that nothing could be gained without work. Money for weekend outings had its price: washing cars, cutting grass, trimming the hedges, weedkilling, household repairs (every family had the right tools in the basement) and in the winter, shoveling snow from the driveway.

The younger son, for example, delivered newspapers around the neighborhood early in the morning (remember the cold Cleveland winter) before going to school, and saved the money to devote to the 'pleasures' corresponding to his age group.

I am referring to the sons of the Chief of Thoracic and Cardiovascular Surgery of the Cleveland Clinic, a man well-placed in society. Understand me well, this was the dominating philosophy in most American homes at that time without class distinction. I remember that one of the residents told me that from high school onwards he would work at two jobs during his vacations, 16 hours a day, to pay for his studies.

I am convinced that the evolution of the consumer society has slowly and progressively deteriorated the youth of our time, both within and outside the United States, with the exceptions to any general rule. The "easy way out" is one of the principal characteristics which increases in proportion to the economic status of the family to which the young person belongs. To this we can add lack of responsibility, lack of individual, family and social compromise, and lack of ideals and utopias.

These are not mere suppositions on my part. My cumulated experience in the secondary colleges to which I am frequently invited to talk with young people is absolutely negative. How I suffer on leaving the classrooms! Cheap materialism has invaded their souls. It is clear to me that the primary responsibility lies with us, the adults. The transformation will come about if we can produce substantial changes in education, starting with television. Children must not only study the usual subjects; here and now it is fundamental for them to analyze today's society without any hindrance, with absolute liberty and active participation in the search for adequate solutions leading to a better world with fewer injustices. Above all they must learn that the fact that they exist signifies a continuous compromise which ends only with death. There will always be time for the enjoyment of daily pleasures if we do not stray from the lessons of Nature, which does not require artificial aids.

Scully was returning to Hawaii at the end of June and despite having worked with him for only a few months felt that I should do something to thank him for the help he had given me. He had been very generous to me and had dedicated a lot of time so that I could progress as rapidly as possible. His advice had been of inestimable value. I asked

Al if it would be possible to hold a barbecue in his house, this of course not being feasible in our apartment. I arranged everything and we said good-bye to him with charcoal-grilled lamb in the best American barbecue style. The day before, we prepared chimichurri, which is a mild piquant sauce typical of Argentina and this lent a taste to the meal which delighted everyone. Toni prepared empanadas which we cooked in the oven. These are made from a mixture of minced beef, chopped fried onion, red peppers, olives, hard-boiled egg, and raisins all wrapped up in a pastry envelope.

Parisi took over the job of Chief Resident and as the workload increased two new "juniors" were incorporated. The operations using the Vineberg technique were on the increase, but the most significant development in the second semester was the introduction of the Starr-Edwards prosthetic valve used to replace deteriorated aortic or mitral valves, principally as a result of rheumatic fever. Although we continued to perform mitral commisurotomies, that is to say forcible opening of the valve without use of extracorporeal circulation, and some attempts at decalcification of aortic valves with the use of the heart-lung machine, once the patient was connected to the pump it became obvious that some valves were impossible to repair and the patient would benefit only by valve replacement. The Starr-Edwards valve was a modification of the Harken design and was the first valve to become generally available to the surgeon. The first surgeons to use it, beside Albert Starr who was its creator, were Effler and Groves.

The main complication we encountered in the first 25 patients was infection, particularly *Staphylococcus aureus*. The valve is a metal cage housing a Silastic ball, and represents a foreign body incapable of defending itself from attack, unlike the tissues of the human body. We learned that it was necessary to administer antibiotics as a preventive measure, starting during the surgery itself via the extracorporeal circulation. Once this cause of death had been removed, the hospital mortality rate declined significantly in the next 25 patients operated on. Valve replacement became a frequent procedure and we gradually learned all its secrets. I followed up each case in detail and was able to present later a paper with 393 replacements to the Ohio Heart Association, which gained me one of the prizes awarded to residents. Effler was present at the prize-giving, which was for me a great privilege. At last we got to September. I sat for my exam and six weeks later received the glad news that I had passed. That afternoon I went to Desk 91, where Eleanor was the first to hear the news. A few minutes later I presented the certificate to Effler. By this time I was more than just a simple "observer" to him. Our relationship went beyond a strictly professional one and it seemed that we had known each other for a long time. He was tremendously delighted and told me what steps to follow. Leedham had been replaced in Education, which made things easier. I was thus able to regularize my situation and became a "junior fellow," which implied countless new responsibilities but at the same time opened a new road to travel along which, if followed with the right objectives and enthusiasm, could lead to great satisfaction. The experience accumulated to date would be of great value and I felt sufficiently well-prepared, but must confess that the excitement that permeated my soul caused me to plan incessantly, even during the night, the task before me, in order that I might reap the greatest benefits.

Without any doubt I felt happy. I was once more confronted by a challenge. Those who know me well, my colleagues in particular, know that I cannot live without challenges. They have been a constant feature of my life and when they are no longer present it will be the moment for me to go.

December was a special month. In the United States the end of year festivities, especially Christmas, start to be celebrated with some weeks of anticipation. Even in November it is common to hear "How are you preparing? what plans do you have? have you decorated your house? have you been shopping? will you be with your relatives or are you going to take a few days vacation? etc., etc."

The stores compete with their decorations, especially with the enormous trees which have been cut down and transplanted to the storefronts where they are decorated with infinite variety. To me it was very sad to see them dead within a few weeks. Inside the stores, all is transformed and the diverse representations of Santa Claus compete with plants and flowers, especially the poinsettias and chrysanthemums. The air is inundated with carols, all contributing to the "Christmas Spirit."

The neighbors decorate the fronts of their homes according to the architectural details, and the carefully arranged lights are particularly memorable. Inside the houses, an important place is given to the Christmas tree which is a real tree cultivated by the million for just that purpose and can be purchased in any supermarket or nursery.

During these weeks the newspapers are full of advertisements for an infinity of products. Pages and pages are dedicated to offering just about anything, all perfectly orchestrated. It is evident that the religious sentiments associated with Christmas take second place, demoted by all this festive fever which has but one purpose: to sell, sell, and sell. In January the statistics appear in all the media announcing that a new record has been reached. Well, it is all part of the consumer society.

For us it was the first Christmas we were to spend away from the family. Once more we would experience nostalgia. I remembered Christmas with my grandmother Cesarea. The table was piled with food, mostly the produce of her garden, lovingly prepared by her own hands, including the traditional sweet cakes called *pan dulce* which she baked in the old clay oven, each of her grandchildren receiving his own as an expression of the love she lavished on us. This feeling of family was always present at Christmas, simple but profound, where ordinary events became important ones because of the sentiments surrounding them. How distant this seemed!

We accepted Vicente's invitation to spend Christmas Eve in his home with other Argentine families. As always we shared the work of preparing for the festivities. It was the custom - at least for the Italian families living in Cleveland- that on Christmas Eve we should eat fish. I proposed cooking cod with polenta, a porridge made from ground maize. Not everyone agreed with this, but I assured them that they would not be disappointed. In Cleveland it was possible in those days to buy Canadian whole dried cod, better than the more customery Norwegian variety due to its thicker and whiter meat and lower salt content which meant less time left in water to soften it by soaking. The recipe is a traditional one from Tuscany. Onions are chopped and fried for a few minutes over a slow fire in good-quality oil. Tomatoes are added, cut into small chunks, the right quantity of tomato paste, fresh red peppers sliced into strips a centimeter wide, salt, pepper, and ground chili. The cod is cut into small pieces and added to the sauce, which is then left to simmer for about 45 minutes. We thus arrived at Vicente's house with two saucepans which caused quite some curiosity. I cooked the polenta in a large saucepan which María provided. At the right moment, we heated the cod and served the meal from the pans, first the polenta and then on top the cod with its sauce. We had bought a good provolone cheese in Alesci's which could be grated and spread over the meal by those who liked this variant. At first, there were some cautious tastings but two empty saucepans at the end of the meal, despite our having prepared an abundant quantity, were testimony to our success. In this way, Grandma Cesarea had at least been with us in spirit. We called our parents by phone and were united with them again in time if not in space.

2

Gaining Confidence
Consolidation

So that the reader can get an idea of what it was like to be a "junior" I shall describe the tasks he was obliged to carry out: He must be present in the operating room every morning at 7 o'clock; every 48 hours he is the doctor on duty, and so when surgery is over he must immediately go to Admissions where the newly-arrived patients are checked in. There, he must note the personal details of each new patient and the rooms to which they have been assigned, then begin his tour of the hospital to check on the progress of all patients under the care of the department, but not located in the department's designated sector. He must pay close attention to the patients to be operated on the next day, and if any detail is missing, usually a laboratory result, solve the problem as soon as possible. Then he must check on the patients who were due for discharge, and go to the eighth floor to the Department of Radiology to separate the preoperative and postoperative films. At about 5 p.m. the general rounds would begin on the eighth floor, and every-one was expected to be present. The X-ray films were then analyzed under the watchful and critical eye of Effler before going down one floor to the Pediatric section where the patients with congenital malformations were located and then floor by floor the junior would present each case in turn. The rounds finished on the second floor with an examination of the patients in the Intensive Care Unit. From that moment onward the junior was left in charge of everything. He had to go back floor by floor and to write the preoperative instructions in detail, including those zones to be shaved, discharge patients, and write a brief account in the case history including recommendations and medication, examine the new patients and note the most recent developments in their case histories. Of course, these tasks could be interrupted at any moment if the junior's presence was required in the Intensive Care Unit, or if he was called to consult with a colleague in another department.

As you can see, there was no time for rest. To minimize the chance of making a mistake, I wrote down all preoperative and postoperative orders in a notebook, and carried a guide to new admissions and a model report for discharge of patients. Most times I did not get to sleep, especially if some patient was unstable following surgery. Of course, it was necessary to call the chief Resident at the slightest doubt and we could always count on the help of the cardiology Fellows in the event of an arrhythmia appearing during recuperation.

Each of us carried a white filing card for each patient, clipped together in the order of visiting them during the afternoon rounds. Every morning before the daily tasks began, the Resident on duty would meet with all his colleagues and go through the cards. Those corresponding to discharged patients would be removed and the cards for the newly admitted patients, which had been written by the duty Resident for distribution to each one of the others, would be incorporated. The Resident going off duty would make detailed comments on any important event of the previous day. That is how we worked as a team, and each of us was expected to know the history of every patient in detail. After going off duty, the Resident went to the operating room to begin his daily tasks and only returned to his home to rest after the usual afternoon rounds. In my own case I made great efforts to ensure that not even the smallest error was committed during my duty period. In general, I would try to make additional rounds on the patients if the work in the Intensive Care Unit permitted it, in order to be absolutely sure that the written account and orders were completely as they should be. My white filing cards were double-sized to have a more complete summary of the case history. It was common for me to respond before the American residents to any question asked by Effler or Groves, even though I was not necessarily on duty.

As you can see, postgraduate education in the United States is organized and very demanding. On graduating from medical school the young physician may take the National Board exam, recognized in many states for medical licensure. After a year of obligatory internship he is permitted to practice medicine. If he wishes to specialize he may take a residency, of variable duration depending on the specialty. To qualify as a cardiologist he must first qualify in internal medicine - four years - and then in cardiology, three years more. If he is inclined towards thoracic and cardiovascular surgery he must follow the residency in general surgery - four years - and then in thoracic and cardiovascular surgery - two or three years. He is then qualified to practice in his speciality but must still take the State Board exam, unless he has passed the National Board and the state accepts the credentials of that exam.

There is a clear difference between this system and that in Argentina where despite some residencies providing adequate training, the majority of physicians qualifying in medicine are permitted to practice immediately, including all imaginable specialities. This contributes yet another irresponsibility to the many which require correction.

I am absolutely convinced that we must redesign our native educational system. Complete reform of the university is required. The first reform was made in 1918, and its content has now almost been forgotten. It is vital to push ahead with a second reform to bring the university up to present-day requirements. We cannot afford to lose any more time.

The salary received by the Residents was just sufficient. It was especially difficult for those Residents with wives and children. They had to make real sacrifices to continue with their studies. It was quite an event to go to a restaurant for a meal, usually reserved for once-a-year celebrations such as a wedding anniversary, or to go to a football or baseball game. Some confessed that the last part of the month was pure hot-dog and Campbell's soup.

The members of the surgical staff were provided by the Clinic twice a year with white shoes of excellent quality leather, and the Residents would always insist that the old shoes not be thrown away, because they could be dyed and continue to be used for a good while. All of these sacrifices would be amply compensated after graduation and beginning to work in the chosen speciality.

My previous experience as a general surgeon, especially during my time in Aráuz, was of great value during these early years. For example, a 40-year old male patient was referred to us with a diagnosis of empyema in his left side - that is to say that he had an accumulation of pus in his thoracic cavity which had produced a collapse of the lung on the same side. The treatment proposed was to open the left side of the chest, aspirate the pus, wash out the cavity, and remove the inflammatory tissue covering the lung so that it would expand. I questioned the patient carefully, and he told me that he had suffered a minor automobile accident some six weeks previously in which he had received a blow to the left side of the chest, without any sign of rib fracture showing on the X-rays which had been taken at the time. Despite the belief that his injuries were minor, he had been given a blood transfusion because of a low hemoglobin. With these facts in mind, I examined him and found a tender mass in the upper left part of the abdomen; even though he had little real pain in the area. He had been discharged a few days after the accident, but then his temperature rose and he was readmitted. My conclusion was that he had a partial rupture of the spleen, and secondary infection. This is termed subphrenic abscess because of its location below the diaphragm, and the pus in the thorax was a consequence of the original site of infection in the abdomen. By operating only in the thorax we would not be able to resolve the problem. I told Effler my conclusions, his answer being; "These South Americans! always thinking about strange things!" At any rate, he bore my observations in mind. As planned, we opened the left side of the thorax, drained the pus, and would obviously have to free the lung, but we noted a bulging in the diaphragm. Effler asked for a large caliber needle and punctured the diaphragm. A creamy pus came up from below, confirming my initial diagnosis. Once we had closed the thorax, we placed the patient in a supine position and made an incision below the ribs on the left side. We aspirated the purulent material, removed the spleen, and drained the abdominal cavity. "At times these South Americans get it right" commented Effler with a sly smile.

On another occasion I was passing through the Intensive Care Unit very early in the morning before going to the operating room. The Resident on duty was worried about a patient who had received an aortic valve replacement the previous day. He had bled more than expected during the night and the Resident suspected cardiac tamponade, which is an accumulation of blood or fluid within the pericardial sac around the heart, leading to compression of the heart and consequent impairment of its function. This would explain the high venous pressure noted by the Resident in the line connected to the patient. He was in favor of an immediate reoperation. My attention was called to the extreme paleness of the patient and the totally collapsed state of his veins, so I checked the line and found a small clot in the three-way stopcock sufficient to block the line and falsely indicate a high pressure. Once the clot had been removed, the true state of his venous pressure was observed to be extremely low. What he needed was urgent replacement of lost blood and not reoperation. We requested two units from the blood bank and the patient's blood pressure returned to normal after he received the transfusion. I have many similar anecdotes, which all go to show that good clinical judgment should always be placed above technology.

Occurrences such as these undoubtedly helped me to move up little by little within the group. I spent a lot of time with the patients. The development of the various medical specialties means that the patients, following admission, will be seen by various physicians and as a result, medicine becomes fragmented and depersonalized. For example, a patient with a cardiac problem will initially be seen by the clinical cardiologist, but in addition to the routine radiological and laboratory tests will be subjected to a variety of additional diagnostic studies: stress testing, nuclear studies, ambulatory electrocardiography, echocardiography (sound wave testing), cine angiography, etc., etc., as indicated by the disease and its complications. Finally he will be examined by a surgeon if surgery is indicated. Without doubt this is all for the good of the patient, but after having been shunted around the hospital and having seen so many faces, he is dazed and confused and may have exchanged only a few words with each intervening physician. I had detected this state of affairs early on and was convinced that it was one of the major defects of American medicine, so efficient but somewhat impersonal. For a country doctor who was accustomed to talking with his patients this was especially evident. I could not lose my old habits and so dedicated a bit more time to them. One example will suffice to explain my views. A Chicago lawyer was sent to the Clinic because of a tumor in his lung. He was seen in the Pulmonary Department and we were consulted principally because bronchoscopy was required. During the afternoon rounds, Dr. Groves interviewed the patient...

"Are you Mr. X?"

"Yes," replied the patient.

"Well, tomorrow we will perform a bronchoscopy."

"As you wish, doctor."

The next day the cytologist confirmed the presence of a malignant tumor. The dialogue continued during the rounds the next afternoon ...

"Well, you know that you have a tumor?"

"Yes doctor, but what type of tumor?"

"A malignant one. It should be removed."

In the United States, the patient is generally told about the type of tumor even if it is a cancer. The dialogue ended like this...

"If you are in agreement we will operate."

"Of course, doctor."

This seemed too cold, so after rounds I went back to see the patient and as I had suspected he was very preoccupied. He had been nominated as a judge, which had been his desire for many years. He had a well-constituted marriage, yet at this moment of great happiness cancer had been discovered during the routine medical examination required by the nomination. For him this could change everything. I explained that the tumor was small, that no complications were evident, and that I was convinced that it could be definitively eradicated by the surgery, the condition having been detected at an early stage of development by the routine examination.

"Do you realize that you have no symptom other than your smoker's cough? You are not spitting blood. You are not in pain. You have not lost weight. Believe me, you should be optimistic. Keep your spirits up!"

"You don't know how grateful I am to you for having given so much time to me," he replied. And so the patients too held me in regard, and I believe would look for me when they needed any points to be clarified

Later on, when working as a Staff member of the Clinic, I personally interviewed every patient sent to me for consultation and developed the habit of making a sketch of the operation planned, usually drawing on a prescription form. Many of them would ask for the drawing so they could later show it to their relatives. Many years afterwards, now settled again in Argentina, I was invited to give a course in Miami. I was interviewed by a local newspaper, and on returning to the hotel that afternoon I called a telephone number in response to a note which someone had left me. To my surprise, it was a patient whom I had operated on for coronary disease years before in Cleveland; he had read my interview in the newspaper. He wished to thank me for having lived all these years and to have been able to celebrate his golden wedding anniversary. "I still have the little drawings you made for me. I want to send them to you as a keepsake. I will send them to the hotel. Eternally grateful, Dr. Favaloro." Before going to dinner, I looked at that paper yellowed by the years that revived happy moments. Medicine practiced without humanity is incomplete.

Indirect revascularization using the Vineberg technique continued to expand. It had been shown that several months were necessary for the development of communicating vessels between the internal mammary artery implant and the coronary circulation; after a sufficient lapse of time the patients were restudied. In the majority the artery was still open and a significant proportion were receiving that extra flow of blood they so desperately needed. As a result, the number of patients requiring mammary artery implant increased month by month.

The Residents, in addition to receiving permission to attend meetings or congresses related to their specialty, had two weeks vacation every year. Right from the start I used this time to visit other centers of cardiovascular surgery. My first trip was to Boston, driving the Valiant, in order to get to know Harvard and especially to meet Dwight Harken who, with his operations performed during World War II to extract projectiles lodged in the heart and great vessels, had given our specialty a great leap forward; his other achievements included mitral commissurotomy. In addition, Robert Gross was working in the Children's Hospital. He was the first in the world to ligate a patent ductus arteriosus and was the innovator of numerous techniques for the repair of congenital defects. Effler was on excellent terms with Harken and gave me a letter of introduction to be presented to him. This was not the case for Dr. Gross who, he told me, was a strange individual difficult to communicate with.

The drive to Boston was extremely pleasant, for it was the autumn of '63. We love to travel by automobile, because if one drives at a moderate speed and escapes every now and again from those freeways which abound in the United States there are many sights to see if one knows how to look carefully.

Fall, especially in northeast United States, is one of the most beautiful sights Nature has to offer. With the arrival of the first cold weather the sap begins to slow down and the leaves display an infinite variety of colors from yellow-green to yellow, ochre, rose, vivid red, and violet depending on the species of bush or tree. Having travelled to almost every corner of the world, I can testify that such a symphony of colors is only to be found in the U.S. and particularly in the northeast. We stopped several times, having left Cleveland on Saturday morning with time to spare, and experienced the ecstasy of the immense forest and its array of tints which continuously changed as we looked from one point to another. Occasionally the enchantment was intensified by the flocks of birds preparing for their annual migration.

On Monday morning I went to the Peter Bent Brigham Hospital in search of Dr. Harken, gave the letter to his secretary, and a few minutes later, full of emotion, I was standing in front of one of the great pioneers of cardiovascular surgery. He received me in a kindly way, speaking while waving his arms about in all directions. It seemed that he could not keep still even for a moment. He told me that the day's tasks would begin with the morning rounds of all his patients, and operations would begin at mid-morning. That afternoon we would go to another hospital, the Mount Auburn, where he operated on a more select group of patients.

I was surprised at the extraordinary friendliness of the man, but soon found that this was part of his character and was extended to all his colleagues and visitors. During rounds it became apparent that he received patients from many different countries in addition to Americans. We eventually went to the surgical suite, his hyperactivity and reddening of face becoming even more accentuated as he scrubbed up. In later years I told him that on this first occasion he had seemed to me to be like a bull pawing the ground at the start of a bullfight. He said that this was perfectly possible, his father having been a cattle breeder and having even sent some bulls to Argentina.

His great experience was very evident in the operating room. Most of his patients were valvular cases and he frequently reoperated on patients with mitral valve disease, a condition with which he undoubtedly had the greatest experience in the world.

After midday, we drove to his home and I was introduced to his wife, Anne, who was obviously very accustomed to receiving visitors. She prepared a light lunch while Harken looked at his letters, especially the international correspondence, with the help of a secretary who worked in the house. After lunch we left for Mount Auburn where he operated, in my view, in better-organized conditions than in Peter Bent Brigham.

On this trip I learned an endless list of things, among them the approach via the right ventricle for a very particular condition - dynamic subaortic stenosis. But most of all it meant for me the beginning of a friendship with someone who merited my deepest respect, not only for his pioneering work but also for his solid academic activity and the ethical lines upon which he ran his professional life.

Dr. Gross began work very early in the morning, which meant that I could go to watch him before reporting to the Peter Bent Brigham. It was extremely difficult to locate him. Although the building in which he operated was easy enough to find, on entering I was treated with total indifference. There was even a feeling that they feared Dr. Gross, because when I explained that I had come from the Cleveland Clinic to observe his operations I received vague replies and evasions. Finally I approached two Residents and asked them, almost begged them, to show me where he entered the building and, as I would not recognize him, to indicate his arrival. This seemed to be acceptable. As soon as he passed through the doorway I approached him and told him of my interest in his work. He asked me to take a seat and wait a few minutes, at the end of which he reappeared already changed for work. He handed me a pair of binoculars and told me to climb a stairway which gave access to the glass ceiling of the operating room. He assured me that I would have a good view of all the details of the surgery from there. "A neat way of getting rid of me," I thought as I climbed the spiral staircase which led me to a roof space fitted with a large oval window in its center, a protective balcony and circular seats around it. To my great surprise, Dr. Gross was absolutely right. With the help of the binoculars it seemed as though I was participating in the surgery just like another assistant. As I was the only observer present during that time, I could move freely around the chamber to find the best angle and note down all the most significant details. When the operations ended and I wanted to clear up some point I would rapidly go downstairs, wait for Gross to emerge, and ask the relevant questions. To my surprise and also I suspected to that of his colleagues as well, he answered with precision and occasionally asked me for my notebook to sketch the stages of the procedure which I was unsure about. What most impressed me was the use of a transverse incision in the anterior wall of the right ventricle to repair interventricular defects and some cases of the tetralogy of Fallot, thus avoiding damage to the muscle fibers. On my return to Cleveland it cost me a lot to convince Effler of the benefits of this approach.

These first two weeks outside the Cleveland Clinic were of immense value and confirmed what I had always thought and practiced during my training as a general surgeon; it is very important to visit other hospitals from time to time to compare and evaluate the good and the bad aspects of the different approaches to our work. I have never stopped learning from other surgical centers.

Another visit I made was to the Mayo Clinic where in the old St. Mary's hospital I could compare the fine and detailed work of Kirklin with the skillful movements of McGoon. I also had a chance to see the membrane oxygenator in use. This was the most efficient device available in those days; it permitted surgeons to keep the patient supported by extracorporeal circulation for long periods of time without undue damage to the blood.

At the end of June Al Parisi finished his residency with the affection and esteem of all of us. He had worked responsibly and was qualified to practice his specialty without problems thanks to the experience he had accumulated.

At that time physicians graduating from prestigious institutions were much sought after, particularly in specialties of continuous evolution and development such as cardiovascular surgery. Requests would be made to Dr. Effler as early as January or February for positions to be filled in July. Al had various options which not only guaranteed his participation in already established groups but also economic tranquility from the start. He had an extremely tempting offer from Pennsylvania, but this did not change his decision to return to his birthplace, Hamilton near Toronto, in fulfillment of a promise he had made to his father who had since died. As a good Sicilian he had to keep his promise, knowing that he would have to start from scratch on a service that at that time only operated on peripheral vascular cases.

Adeline was happy to return to Hamilton where her parents had missed her sorely, she being their only child. Little by little, Al successfully built up a new center for cardiac surgery. We spoke frequently by telephone, mainly because he referred the more complicated cases to us at the beginning, thus demonstrating yet again his sense of responsibility. There would be time in the future to operate on them locally without problems once the service was organized fully.

One Friday night in the middle of winter he called me as he often did. I thought that his call would be about some patient, but unfortunately this was not the case: "René, Adeline has died." For some time, difficult to calculate under these circumstances, his sobs and mine intermingled despite the distance.

"Al, what happened? Tell me."

"As you know, Adeline was expecting our fourth child, due in something less than two months. Her varices were bothering her and a mild phlebitis appeared a few days ago. I went to the hospital as usual very early and she stayed in bed. In the middle of the morning I was called and told that she had been found dead in the bathroom." We concluded that a thrombus (blood clot) had detached from one of her varicose veins and had produced a massive pulmonary embolism.

Toni and I decided to attend the funeral. The journey from Cleveland to Hamilton by way of Buffalo was a drive of some 300 miles on the freeway, which could be done in a little more than four hours if it were not for the winter conditions. We left on Sunday early in the morning and arrived at the parlor before midday. Our meeting with Al and the family of Adeline was tremendously painful. I do not believe I have ever seen another funeral like this one. There was almost continual sobbing. In the United States and Canada the funerals take place a number of days after the demise, to allow time for relatives and friends to arrive from distant parts. For this reason the body is usually embalmed. Toni did not wish to see Adeline, and Al accompanied me. Adeline was lying there as though asleep. The custom is to apply makeup to hide the appearance of death and return the face to a more natural color. At first this produced in me a disagreeable sensation and seemed not natural, but later I concluded that it was perhaps a way of leaving those closest to the deceased with a lasting lifelike impression.

The funeral parlor had a dining room and there we ate a frugal lunch with Al and his mother, in order to be together and a little more removed from such a tragic scene.

"Can you imagine, René, now that I am in a position to give her a few of the things we never had - you remember how we lived in Cleveland - she has gone forever." This was true. During Al's residency she had been restricted to cooking, washing, ironing, sewing, mending, and looking after the children she loved so much.

We stayed until the evening and returned along the freeway almost without speaking, faced with weather hazards. Although only a little snow had fallen, the temperature had dropped abruptly and it was like driving on an ice rink. It took a long time to get home. I could not stop over because of the heavy surgical schedule waiting for me on Monday.

Franklin Bichlemeier of Kansas had replaced Al as Senior Resident. The workload increased so much that for the first time in the service it was necessary to increase the number of Fellows and to appoint two Seniors to share the tasks.

In 1964, I was Chief Resident, and the Clinic sent me to Houston to Dr. Denton Cooley's service to see if the new bubble oxygenator was of any value and if it could be used for our patients. Our workload was increasing and the time-consuming task of setting up and later disassembling and cleaning our own oxygenator meant that it was virtually impossible to operate on two patients the same day. The new oxygenator was based on an old principle used by Dr. Walton Lillehei which was to oxygenate the blood by bubbling oxygen through it. The device was disposable, a real revolution. Kolff gave me very precise instructions about what I should observe and provided me with a form for each patient on which I would note the details of the patient such as age, weight, disease, perfusion time, pH, oximetry, free hemoglobin, urine production, etc. I was expected to present a detailed report on my return.

Effler and Cooley were great friends, and the moment arrived when all had been arranged for my trip. As usual our plan was to travel by car. Effler thought I was crazy. It was difficult to make him understand that the Argentines are accustomed to travelling long distances and that to pass by 700 or 800 miles in the U.S. in one day was easy using the freeway system. The trip was uneventful. To travel through Texas, especially the northeast part, was like travelling through our Pampas. Cattle could be seen everywhere, very different from those thin longhorned cattle we used to see in the cowboy movies. The crosses with Brahman, Charolais and Hereford were evident to the connoisseur, which I had become a long time before.

Cooley received me with open arms, because he did not have enough Residents at that time. I worked without interruption from seven in the morning to the early hours of the evening. I helped him in virtually all of his operations. Cooley worked in two operating theaters and ran from one to the other without losing a single moment, his organization being perfect. I could verify that his fame as an extraordinary surgeon was justified: his manual ability permitted him to transform the most complicated surgical maneuvers into simple movements, and this resulted in faster operations. The diseases seen by him were most varied, with the exception of coronary atherosclerosis which he did not know well due to the poor quality of the coronary cineangiography in Houston. My work was therefore two-fold: to participate in the operations and to check the details of the extracorporeal circulation so I could fill in my forms and prepare the final report. I even had to act as a translator when Cooley was interviewed by Panamanian television.

In conclusion, my final report was that the device was a success, the only exception being its use in large and heavy patients who could suffer inadequate oxygenation. As a result the bubble oxygenator began to be utilized in our surgical department.

A few days after my return, Effler showed me a letter sent to him by Cooley in which he praised my work in Houston. He emphasized my capacity for work, and in one of the regular heavy-humored comments which he and Effler used to interchange finished by saying that it had been a pleasure for him to have put the final polish on my surgical skills!

During my period as Chief Resident I took care of the activities of the Department down to the smallest detail, helped the "juniors" in any way I could, delegating tasks to them as part of their training, but at the same time watching over them closely, and providing them with an example through total dedication, hard work, effort, and responsibility. To give the reader an idea, it was usual for the Residents on duty to take a rest, when time allowed, on the eighth floor.

The Intensive Care Unit was on the second floor. The nurses knew that if an emergency arose, such as a cardiac arrest, they were to call me in addition to calling the Resident. As I have mentioned, I lived in the Palais Royal just across the street. Instead of using pyjamas I would sleep in the green top and trousers we used for surgery. On being called, I could then jump directly out of bed, throw on a cape which was always at hand, and run over to the Hospital. In this way I could usually arrive in the unit before the "junior."

I already explained that only Dr. Groves was authorized to cannulate the patients. We would open the thorax and then wait for his arrival. One day I said to Effler that I thought the time had come for the Residents to cannulate, and so from 1964 onwards we were authorized to do so. I remember that in one of the earliest cases, a patient with severe mitral valvular disease and a greatly enlarged right atrium and inferior vena cava (in those days we used an approach via the right side of the chest), on beginning to dissect the union of the vena cava with the right atrium I accidently caused a large rent in the posterior wall. My first thought was: "Say goodbye to cannulations." Fortunately, I was able to repair the wall with some difficulty.

Effler arrived a few minutes later and replaced the valve with no problems. After he had finished and was about to leave, I asked him to have a look at the posterior wall. He found the sutures and I confessed what had happened. He looked at me and said: "That's one way of learning. I hope it is not repeated." We continued to cannulate.

As Chief Resident I got to do a lot of surgery: ductus, coarctations, a few Blalocks, pulmonary resections, esophageal repairs, mediastinal tumors, atrial septal defects, and some valve replacements. All this in addition to a large number of mammary artery dissections and Vineberg implants. I thus could not complain about how my training was progressing, on the contrary I was very satisfied and more so for the guidance and help given to me by Effler and

Groves who assisted in my first operations.

I cannot leave untold an anecdote which will contribute to a fuller portrait of Effler. One morning we were doing an aortic valve replacement in one of the most important members of the Jewish community of Cleveland. The operation went ahead perfectly normally but at the end we found it impossible to defibrillate and restart the heart, try as we would with the internal defibrillator. After many attempts, Effler left the operating theater to speak with the relatives. By that time I was familiar with the solution of Sodi Pallares, a distinguished cardiologist of the Mexican Instituto de Cardiología; the solution was composed of glucose in high concentration, potassium, and insulin. I asked for these ingredients to be brought to me, made the solution on the spot and injected it slowly into the root of the aorta. For the first time the heart defibrillated and began beating normally, but after a few minutes fibrillated again. I injected a second dose and this time the heart could be defibrillated and continued to beat with ever increasing force, allowing us finally to wean the patient off the extracorporeal circulation. In those days we did not routinely measure the blood potassium during perfusion, and it could sometimes fall to low levels. I am sure that, on that occasion, the success of the Sodi Pallares solution was due to its high content of potassium. Effler appeared at the door and told us that the family had been informed of our failure. When I told him what had happened he scrubbed up again and came in to confirm with his own eyes and hands that our story was true. He thanked us and went to tell Mrs. Lovemann what had happened, giving me full credit for her husband's recovery. Mr. Lovemann continued to live for many more years, the Clinic receiving regular donations from him and I, once in a while, dozens of the best steaks!

The same type of thing happened in the case of a little girl Effler operated on for a high ventricular septal defect, which he repaired without problems using a patch. When he was about to close the ventricle I told him that I suspected another defect lower down because red blood was still getting to the right ventricle. This was indeed the case and was easily repaired. Effler told the family the whole story. As you can see, it was not just cardiovascular surgery we learned at his side.

My period as Chief Resident came to its close, and with it my training and graduation as a cardiovascular surgeon. I told Effler of my desire to return home to Argentina. He tried to dissuade me and keep me at his side, but in vain. In the middle of 1965 we returned to La Plata with the idea of contributing my acquired knowledge to the development of cardiovascular surgery in our country. It was wonderful to be back with our families and friends again and after enjoying their company for a few days I began my pilgrimage. In Buenos Aires there were two cardiovascular surgery groups which I visited a number of times to exchange ideas and discuss the possibility of my incorporation. It was obvious that the work they were doing was far different from ours in the United States. Despite all my efforts, they showed little interest. As in the case of so many Argentine physicians trained abroad, instead of thinking that the acquisition of new knowledge and techniques could be a positive contribution to better health care, the new arrival was looked on from an egoist's point of view as a competitor who would eclipse and then displace the locals, who had no idea of what it was like to work as a team.

There was the remote possibilty of starting a cardiovascular surgery service in the Children's Hospital of La Plata, but the provincial minister of health at that time was a man from the interior of the country who received me wearing a small poncho over his shoulders and proceeded to speak at length about the social importance of tuberculosis.

Effler wrote to me frequently, and to be absolutely sure of my receiving his letters he would mail a duplicate two or three days later. Finally we had to admit our disillusion and we returned to Cleveland. I promised my parents that we would visit them every year, in order to make our parting less traumatic.

Following the offer made to me by Effler in his letters, I was nominated "Assistant Staff" of the Cleveland Clinic with an annual salary of 18 thousand dollars. This category was created for those who had finished their training but wished to continue in order to acquire more experience and with the possibility of being advanced to "staff," which was the name given to the permanent members of the institution. In a long conversation Effler discussed the details of my position in his department. I was free to operate on any patient referred to me. I was given my own office at "Desk 91," which was close to his, and I was given a secretary. The first one was incompetent and was replaced by Candice, who had just left school, and under the guidance of Eleanor gained in experience and was transformed into the ideal collaborator always prepared to help me in everything despite her heavy workload.

At the same time Effler told me that I would have to sit for my "State Board" examination. A physician graduating in the U.S. cannot start his own practice until he has spent an obligatory year as an intern, and passed the State Board examination required by each state or the National Board examination so that he can be licensed to practice. Most states have reciprocity arrangements so that the successful candidate in one state is recognized in others. This was of great importance in my case because Ohio had stipulated that only American physicians could sit for the examination, which meant that I would have to sit in another state with a reciprocity agreement, and the Clinic would take care of the paperwork later. Once more I would have to waste time studying subjects which had little to do with my specialty. Finally, Effler added: "René, you will have to move out of that fleapit of yours and find a decent place to live in."

The Cleveland Clinic was indeed located in a district in which robberies, assaults, and street accidents were frequent. Almost all of the residents were black and lived in run-down buildings that often lacked central heating. Few were employed, and many of the rest lived off casual work. It was common to see them around the numerous bars or wandering drunk and aimlessly about the streets, almost always begging. The children were testimony to the world in which they lived. They looked thin and emaciated, badly dressed, and their sad faces were pitiful. This was the reality of our barrio. Of course, they did not represent the general black population. There were a number of respectable districts in which black people lived no different from the majority of the whites.

We were able to prove to ourselves that this was not just a problem of Cleveland. All large American cities had areas like this. It is incorrect to believe that America is a bed of roses. About 40 million people, the majority of them black, live in poverty, are underfed, lack medical care and access to a good education. The shanty towns are not the exclusive property of Latin America. This is not the moment to analyze the reasons why, but it is evident that the consumer society is not the whole answer. It is, on the contrary, full of errors which must be resolved in some later stage of man's evolution. We must all be conscious of this and contribute to a better world, preserving liberty but at the same time correcting injustices. I am firmly convinced that the correct way can only be found through education.

What Effler did not know is that despite all his admonitions to the contrary, we often went out walking. Just past 105th Street there was a beautiful park which extended from Euclid to Lake Erie. In spring and summer it was flooded with flowers among the luxuriant trees. The art museum was a favorite place where we always found something new to arouse our interest.

A little further to the east, but still in the park, was

Severance Hall, the home of the Cleveland Orchestra. Even as a child I was attracted to classical music, which I heard on the radio, and was attentive to the commentaries of my father who had been a violinist as well as a cabinet maker. His friends used to say that his old maestro, Professor Laghman, considered him to be his best disciple. The violin had been put away when his mother had died, 40 days after my birth. One day during my adolescence I summoned up courage and asked him: "Father, I have never heard you play the violin. Why don't you play it now, even for a few minutes?" He thought about it for a while, then got out the violin which he lovingly tuned stroking it with the bow and then played pieces of various works, his look lost I don't know where. It was the first and last time. I have always regretted, more with the passage of the years, never having learned to play the instrument. The old violin is now restored waiting for one of his great grandchildren to break its silence. At least I hope so.

During those years, the Cleveland Orchestra under the baton of George Szell was considered to be the most important in the United States. Lovers of music, we would attend the concerts frequently, most times with tickets given to us by patients, and listen to the perfection of the performances. Szell was demanding, conducted with an economy of movement, more with his look than his hands and when some small mistake was made his countenance would become transformed and menacing. So it was that for years during fall and winter we had the opportunity of not only enjoying the Orchestra but also the invited soloists such as Rubinstein, David and Igor Oistrakh, and above all Rostropovich. I will always remember his first visit to Cleveland when he played the concerto written for him by Shostakovitch. The public virtually deified him at the end of the perfomance, with a long standing ovation. Alone or accompanied by Szell, Rostropovich returned to the platform innumerable times, finishing with a grand embrace with Szell. He thanked the audience with tears in his eyes and played a brief encore. He was still living in Russia at that time, and what occurred in Severance Hall that night was proof that in art and science there are no barriers.

It is difficult to express the infinite variety of sensations I experienced at the concerts of the Cleveland Orchestra. I can only thank Szell, his musicians and soloists for having moved my soul. I find it incomprehensible that the majority of young people these days prefer the infernal noises made by massacred instruments accompanied by guttural howls which pretend to be musical expression. Perhaps this forms part of the general confusion into which they escape to avoid their responsibilities.

We never had any problem in our walks on Euclid, perhaps because we are not blue-eyed and blond-haired, or because we always kept to the main streets, or just out of sheer good luck.

I began this second stage in the Cleveland Cinic with enormous enthusiasm. My daily workload was rapidly increasing; in addition to collaborating with everyone I began to operate on my own patients, and now had the added responsibility of preparing myself for the exam which evidently was going to be much more complicated than the ECFMG. It would take four days, and it would be necessary to pass each of the subjects: anatomy, physiology, biochemistry, clinical medicine, surgery, obstetrics and gynecology, pediatrics, hygiene, and social medicine. Failing in only one subject meant failing the whole exam. I began by finding out which textbooks were used by the students in American medical schools, especially those dealing with the basic sciences which would undoubtedly be the most difficult and demanding of my time. I remember, for example, using Harper for biochemistry.

The day's work in the Clinic finished at about five in the afternoon and every day I would dedicate two or three hours to preparation for the exam before or after the evening meal, and for about three months spent the weekends cloistered with my books which I must admit I hated because they were taking time away from my real job. I fell behind especially in reading the cardiology and cardiovascular surgery journals.

It was a necessary effort. For legal reasons my operations appeared as Effler - Favaloro or Groves - Favaloro in the case histories, even though these two did not participate. For a one-week period both of them were absent and I was for the first time in charge of the Department. For this week, the operations were listed as Hoerr - Favaloro. Dr. Stanley Hoerr was the chairman of the Division of Surgery, we always maintained an excellent relationship with him and he kindly agreed to guard my back.

About that time I was fortunate enough to perform the first successful pulmonary embolectomy in the history of the Cleveland Clinic. Sometimes, for a variety of reasons, clots form in the extremities or abdomen of the patients and later become detached to flow with the blood via the vena cava to the heart where they pass through the cavities of the right side and emerge into the pulmonary artery and its branches which become obstructed by the clots. It is an extremely serious situation which can cause the death of the patient in minutes.

In this particular case the patient had been operated on by Dr. Rupert Turnbull some ten days before as a consequence of Crohn's disease, an inflammatory process affecting mostly the small intestine. Our interpretation of the clinical signs led us to take the patient to the operating theater where he arrived in a very poor hemodynamic state, with a barely detectable blood pressure. During intubation for anesthesia the heart stopped and we had to apply external cardiac massage. We quickly placed femoral arterial and venous catheters in order to start partial extracorporeal circulation. I opened the thorax without wasting time. The sternum acts as a support so that only one slash was required to cut through skin, underlying tissue, and periosteum. The bone was cut with a special saw and did not require control of bleeding. A Finochietto retractor was then positioned, the pericardium opened, and a second venous cannula placed in the right atrium which in these cases is enormously distended. We could thus improve the venous return to the extracorporeal circulation and the surgeon could then relax, the pump having taken over the work of the lungs and heart.

In a few minutes the blood that had been dark blue returned to its normal color, the blood pressure improved and the heart assumed a more normal size. A well-trained team - for this is not a surgeon's job - can put a patient on extracorporeal circulation in less than 10 minutes. This is no exaggeration, we have done this many times for a variety of reasons. It only remained for us to open the pulmonary artery and meticulously extract the thrombi, which in this case were abundant, then close the incision with atraumatic suture and take the patient off the pump. The patient recuperated well. This being the first case of survival following pulmonary embolism, it had a big impact. We presented it in one of the ordinary case meetings and it was published in the Cleveland Clinic Quarterly.

Sewell had introduced a modification of the Vineberg operation. Instead of dissecting only the internal mammary artery itself and separating it from the thoracic wall, which was a very meticulous job, he decided to dissect a pedicle which included the veins, pleura, and muscles. In this way it was possible to avoid touching the artery itself and hence traumatizing it, and also meant much less time spent in the preparation. Effler invited Sewell to operate on a patient in the Cleveland Clinic and I assisted him during the surgery. I carefully observed every stage of the process, for I knew that we almost certainly would have to repeat it. What I did not like was the use of a scalpel with a wide blade to make the tunnel big enough to accept the entire pedicle.

From then on we used Sewell's technique for dissecting the internal mammary artery, but, to avoid a wide tunnel, we prepared the distal portion of the artery by eliminating all surrounding tissue to expose the artery so that the implantation could be made according to the original Vineberg ideas. We termed this combination the Vineberg-Sewell technique and it became standard for all types of implant.

The Boards exam was coming closer, and I studied with ever more earnestness in my free moments. To improve my chances of passing, I registered for it in both Virginia and New York. There was only a fortnight between the two exams and both offered reciprocity with Ohio. When the time came I moved with Toni to Virginia. The sessions occupied both morning and afternoon, starting with the basic sciences. On the second day, after the physiology and biochemistry exams, I told my wife that I was disillusioned and was pessimistic because the questions had little to do with what I had studied. They were exhausting days, not only because of the long hours we spent sitting at a desk, but also because of the psychological pressure we suffered in almost all the subjects. I remember that the professor of gynecology at the University of Virginia, who was in charge of the exam, said a few words before it started: "Dear colleagues, the National Board sent me 360 questions of which I selected the 180 which appeared easiest to me. However, I must confess that I do not know if I myself could pass. Some questions appear to be much too complicated. Don't be disillusioned by what I am telling you. Make a good effort and do the best you can. Good luck!"

After the exam, we returned home. My brain was in a state of confusion, and I did not feel sure of having passed. I was, however, absolutely convinced that this was not the way of finding out if a doctor was capable of exercising his profession. To my way of thinking, the only justification of such a trial was that there was no other way of achieving the same objective given the number of candidates to be tested.

On rejoining the team, Effler asked me how I had fared. I told him that I did not know, but that New York at least represented another chance. A fortnight later I went through the same experience, albeit a little more skilled. I rapidly marked the questions I knew well, and those I did not, so that after this first pass I knew which were the questions to consider carefully.

The results were received in about six weeks. You can imagine my anxiety while waiting for them. At last they came, and I had been successful in both. This surprised me, for I was convinced that I had failed the physiology exam in Virginia. The only explanation was that the 70 percent score needed to pass was not based on absolute terms but on 10 percent of the highest scores recorded in the exams. Whatever the explanation, I felt happy and contented. The only thing left to be completed now was the red tape associated with reciprocity, but most of this was accomplished by the Clinic itself which took charge of preparing my case for official recognition despite my being a foreigner. By now I occupied a definite position in the Clinic and its authorities considered that my work was worthy enough for me to continue.

I was granted the Ohio license, and at the beginning of 1966 I was appointed a Staff member of the Cleveland Clinic. A lot of things had happened since that February of 1962! I was proving yet again that to my way of thinking the only road of getting somewhere is through dedication, working without limits, responsibility, and the honesty with which the work is carried out. Without this, possession of a few neurones is of small value.

When a new member of the Staff is nominated in the Cleveland Clinic, the Board of Governors - which is the ultimate authority of the institution, elected by the vote of its members - notifies all medical staff. I was happy to discover that the majority had approved my appointment. Everywhere I went I was told of this in one form or another. It goes without saying that in addition to Effler and Groves, the members of the Department of Cardiology with Sones and Proudfit at its head were the first and most effusive, also Al Humphries and Ed Beven who were in charge of Peripheral Vascular Surgery and with whom I had so much in common.

In the Cleveland Clinic peripheral vascular surgery, which comprises the carotid arteries, abdominal aorta, and the vessels of the legs, constituted a separate Department led by Alfred Humphries with Edwin Beven as his associate. In most hospitals this work is done by the cardiac surgeons, as we do in Argentina.

Al was one of the pioneers of vascular surgery. He had started as an orthopedic surgeon but when the first articles about this new field were published he became interested, and was responsible in our Clinic for many original contributions. He was a talented surgeon who possessed extraordinary manual ability and could work tirelessly. Ed was born in Chile of English parents and had graduated from McGill University in Montreal, later joining the group at the Cleveland Clinic and specializing with Humphries. We established an early friendship which deepened with time. In the few moments I had free between operations I would frequently go to the rooms where Ed and Al were working, attracted by the challenge of vascular surgery. It was in this way that Al Humphries became one of my close friends among the surgical staff, and I would sometimes help them in complicated cases such as the first thoraco-abdominal aneurysms on which they operated.

Crile called and asked me to see him. By then we had formed a deep and sincere friendship. He told me how happy he was that I was now part of the family, but wanted to tell me a few things. The most important was that as a member of the Staff of the Cleveland Clinic I had absolute freedom to work and develop new ideas, that free will was the only pathway to progress. That I should understand that the positions and divisions within the structure of the Clinic were necessary but that he saw in me great potential which should be allowed to develop by my working free of restraints. I thanked him emotionally for his advice and once again learned to value his spiritual grandeur.

It only remained for us to look for a new home. For reasons of necessity we had lived almost in a cage until now and longed for the open spaces of our house in Aráuz. If we really were going to stay, and were sure of what we would be doing in the foreseeable future and perhaps forever, it must be outside of the city. We toured the different areas we had gotten to know in our outings, especially during the short spring and summer. Chagrin Falls, profusely wooded and with few houses, was too far away and Beachwood beyond Warrensville Road was neither city nor country, the houses although detached had been constructed on lots which were too small. We finally looked to Pepper Pike, a residential zone of softly rolling ground and abundant green spaces due to the regulations specifying that each house must be constructed on a lot of at least an acre.

It cost us months to find what we really wanted. Only a few houses came up for sale, until one day we received a call from a real estate agent with whom we had been in contact. He told us he had just what we were looking for. And so it was. The house occupied a two acre lot on the corner of Shaker Boulevard and Bowlingbrook Road. The rear part was on a gentle slope which ended in a small stream which ran diagonally from Bowlingbrook to Shaker. This triangle was densely wooded, especially the part near the stream. The house was of California style and had three floors, but given its location in the center of the lot where the ground began to drop away the main entrance was on the second floor and the rear on the first. The bedrooms were on the third floor. The most striking feature was an enormous living/dining room looking toward the north, and whose walls were of glass except for a large chimney. How we enjoyed the winter heat of the logs burning in the hearth while looking out of the windows at the trees and lawns covered with snow, where the squirrels were almost always busying themselves! To the south, near the stream, was a clearing. I could see myself again as a market gardener!

We rapidly reached an agreement with the owner. How were we going to pay? It is true that we did not have the necessary sum, but in these cases one goes to a bank. It makes an independent evaluation, confirms that the price is reasonable, analyzes the financial status of the buyer (in particular his salary), and grants a long-term credit of some 20 or 30 years at a low rate of interest if the calculations so indicate. The buyer must pay in advance a small portion in relation to the purchase price. That is how we bought it through the bank in which we had opened our first account.

We moved at the end of summer, with the kitchen furniture and a folding bed/sofa to sleep on. Little by little we began to fill the house. That first weekend I explored the entire lot. Undoubtedly the most beautiful part was at the side of the stream where the crystalline water ran quickly down its steeply sloping course. The trees were so dense that only a few rays of sun could penetrate them and illuminate the soil. I could not even see my neighbor's house on the other side of the stream. There was still a large variety of birds, preparing for migration, among which were goldfinches, red cardinals, bluejays, swallows, and the occasional woodpecker. Surprisingly a pair of pheasants emerged from the matted grass and rapidly walked under the bridge spanning Bowlingbrook. In time we saw a lot of them, generally around the stream, and I will always remember one morning on the way to work how the traffic stopped to allow a hen with her brood to leisurely cross the highroad a few blocks from home.

Behind the house and towards the west there were various apple trees, old and uncared for. As I have mentioned there was a clearing of about 30 by 15 yards next to the stream, free of trees and quite sunlit. This would be the place for the kitchen garden.

The first I did was to buy a chainsaw, and the following Saturday I chopped down and converted into logs the majority of the apple trees, which were beyond salvation except for two, one of which was near the kitchen. I piled up the logs near the stream in preparation for the barbecues to come.

The grounds needed looking after, and I put myself to finding the right tools. One of my neighbors was that brilliant vascular surgeon, Al Humphries, who lived on Shaker but a little more east, past Lander Road. He was one of our first visitors, and I took him on a tour of the property, asking his advice on what to buy. He said to me: "Look, I have a complete set of gardening equipment including a tractor, which I have grown tired of using. Come over and pick it all up." I agreed, with one condition: that he sell it to me. He felt obliged to charge me one hundred dollars. During the weekends I would mow the lawn sitting on my tractor, trim the edges, pull weeds, take care of the trees and bushes and above all tend the flower beds with their abundance of plants and flowers surrounding our house.

The change in our style of living was undoubtedly significant. Both Toni and I enjoyed the place enormously. I had to buy her a car, financed of course, in which she could drive about. I was enthusiastic about cultivating my own vegetables as I had done since my childhood when my grandparents had taught me all the secrets. The ground had never been turned over, and half-buried stones of all sizes could be seen everywhere. This would require a large tractor. I had noticed that one of my neighbors who lived in front of us over Bowlingbrook had one. Would he have a plow? It was a matter of asking him. One morning I saw him walking the grounds of his home, so I approached and introduced myself, and explained what I wanted to do following the winter now approaching. He told me that he himself did not have a plow, but a friend of his did and he would do his best to borrow it. The next weekend, Saturday and Sunday, was spent with him plowing and me following behind picking up the stones dislodged by the plow and throwing them into the stream. From time to time we took a break and quenched our thirst with some beers. He refused to accept payment for his help.

My little tractor had a disc harrow with which I finished preparing the ground over the next few days. There were a number of dairy farms near Cleveland, and at one of them I was able to acquire natural manure, a mixture of dung and straw, which I spread over the prepared ground. The snow covered everything during the winter and in the following spring I harrowed the ground once more and sowed everything you could imagine: 100 tomato plants, 50 sweet pepper plants, 50 eggplants, all types of salad including chicory, spinach, carrots, beans, basil, parsley, and even angolan calabashes, a variety of Argentinian pumpkin with seeds sent by my parents. That summer it rained almost every week, so I had to irrigate only a few times. The vegetables developed splendidly in the fertile soil. Obviously my neighbor with the tractor was the first to sample them, but there were so many that all my friends from the Clinic were invited to take their pick whenever they wished. Joanna often appeared during the afternoon, having fallen in love with the soil.

We really took pleasure in the house that first summer. Since it did not grow dark until after nine and I arrived between six and six thirty, we had a couple of hours every day to walk the grounds, observing the flowers, the azaleas, rhododendrons, peonies, and rosebushes, while an infinity of birds sang in the trees looking for roosting places. The cardinals had made their nests in the arborvitae near the main entrance and in the apple tree next to the kitchen. We had hung feeders so that no bird would want for food and later we discovered that some, especially the cardinals, did not migrate if they were treated well. It was only necessary to make sure that they had enough food during the winter when the snow covered everything. On weekends I would often sit in a lounger reading or studying by the stream, accompanied by my own riotous bird orchestra. We also enjoyed the winter. The first snows would begin to fall in December, getting heavier in January and February, and generally not stopping until April. The countryside was transformed by the white blanket of snow and different figures would begin to emerge from the trees and bushes around the house according to the quantity and frequency of the snowfalls and the light and shadow effects of the scarce patches of sunlight.

All of this we watched through the glass walls of the living room, one of my favorite places during the winter when nostalgia would invade our lives. Listening to our own music, preferably our zambas, cuecas, vidalas and chacareras; artists like Atahualpa Yupanqui, Eduardo Falú, Jaime Torres, Ariel Ramirez and others would take me back home. Our native music is so colorful and its poetry, when analyzed with care, is not only beautiful but also transmits the happiness and sorrows of our people. The Misa Criolla, for example, soon became a favorite present for our American friends who would enjoy it immensely even though unable to understand many of the words. I also went back to reading some of my favorite books, including our epic Gaucho poem "Martín Fierro" and "Don Quixote," the poetry of Lugones, Antonio Machado or García Lorca, and the social and historical works of Martinez Estrada, Luis Franco or Julio Irazusta.

I cannot understand how love of reading, especially in the young, has declined so much. My inquiries in the secondary schools - one of my favorite questions when a dialogue begins - reveal that they do not spend time reading. They do not know what they are missing. Reading a good book alone and in silence is one of life's most rewarding pleasures; it enriches our knowledge while filling our spirit with infinite images which give rise to astonishment, analysis, criticism, and reflection. It is also good to read aloud in class or with friends to exchange ideas and opinions.

That is what we did in our youth. We had to read in the National College and were obliged to read at home (I would sometimes choose the woods or a quiet city square) for later comment in class. If I wrote down the list of required reading for the fourth school year it would cause surprise and few of today's youth would believe it possible. Today they waste time with video games or television whose programs, with rare exceptions, serve only to contribute to the general ignorance. I firmly believe that it would be possible to encourage reading through television with programs in which chapters of important books are read and illustrated with examples related to the text. It should not be difficult to do this with the technology presently available.

In spite of living about 20 miles from the Clinic, the route was almost direct and took about half an hour without hurrying. In the last few miles North Park ran through a wooded area with a small lake which froze over during the winter much to the delight of the children who would happily skate on it. These last few miles were full of beauty that changed according to the seasons and always made for a pleasant trip.

My workload continued to increase because in addition to the patients from the Cardiology service run by Bill Proudfit and colleagues, or directly from B10, I began to receive patients referred directly to me by their own doctors especially for revascularization surgery. Even though I continued to operate the whole spectrum of thoracic disease, the numbers of pulmonary resections and esophageal operations began to decline perhaps without my noticing it. Groves preferred to take care of them while for me there were ever more cardiac operations. In addition to valve replacements we were frequently employed in resecting ventricular aneurysms resulting from previous myocardial infarcts. An infarct signifies the death of an area of heart muscle which may be of any size from a small one hardly noticeable during catheterization to large ones which are generally the consequence of occlusion of the anterior descending branch of the left coronary artery near its origin and which destroy much of the wall of the left ventricle. The heart muscle is replaced by scar tissue that slowly undergoes dilation and ends up forming a cavity which generally has clots in its interior. This is what we call an aneurysm, and we learned to remove it by restoring the architecture of the left ventricle. At times they were enormous, occupying the left base of the thoracic cavity and provoking severe symptoms of heart failure.

In those days, the left ventricle was analyzed during catheterization by injecting a significant quantity of contrast medium into its cavity and filming with the patient lying on his side in a position known as right anterior oblique. This allowed us to see the front wall, the apex, and the posterior (diaphragmatic) wall of the left ventricle but did not allow us to see the wall between the two ventricles or the lateral wall. My observations during surgery indicated that these views were also important given that patients who appeared to have the entire ventricular wall destroyed when seen from the right anterior oblique projection often demonstrated an actively contracting lateral wall during surgery, which was fundamental to the improvement of function of the ventricle following removal of the aneurysm. In my talks with Sones I mentioned my concern to him and we began to use an additional projection, the left anterior oblique. Using the two oblique projections we could then achieve a global view of the left ventricle which was of tremendous importance in the selection of the patients to be operated on.

The median anterior incision, which is used to gain access to the thoracic cavity by splitting the sternum longitudinally, offered many advantages: we had direct access to the heart and great vessels, it was quickly done because we did not have to cut muscle, the lungs were subject to less handling, and it was the least painful during the immediate postoperative period. As a consequence it rapidly gained ground over the transverse incision which we originally used. I remember now with horror that we would even perform aortic valve replacements using the old transversal incision.

Once the sternum was open, each side had to be raised carefully to prevent loss of blood, mainly from the periosteum (the membrane covering bone), and then place in position the Finochietto retractor to obtain the appropriate operating field. At the end of the operation we would again check for bleeding this time taking special care after passing through the bone the wires which were used to close the sternal incision.

These manipulations allowed me to observe and to feel the two mammary arteries which ran along the sternum, one on each side, a few centimeters from the incision. I thought that it would be possible to dissect them using this new approach just as easily as we did routinely via the left thoracotomy. In some patients whose condition was stable and uncomplicated immediately following the operation I began to prepare the arteries in small segments generally at the level of the fourth or fifth intercostal space according to the Sewell technique. It turned out to be easy, perhaps easier than using the left thoracotomy. I then concluded that it might be feasible to dissect both mammary arteries and implant them both in the left ventricle of patients with diffuse coronary lesions.

I analyzed this possibility with Mason Sones. He told me that somebody, he did not quite remember who, had stressed that if this were done then bone necrosis would result due to lack of blood supply. This somewhat cooled my enthusiasm but on carefully revising the anatomy it proved to be an unacceptable argument, the sternum receiving blood from other vessels and especially the intercostal arteries. I then set out in search of the ideal patient: he had to be relatively young, to have diffuse coronary lesions but preferably with collaterals, and whose cardiac muscle was in good shape. David Fergusson, a South African cardiologist from Cape Town who was part of Mason Sones' group, had studied just such a patient, of Italian descent and who lived in Florida. He presented the case to me as a candidate for the by now classic operation we were accustomed to doing, but I proposed the double mammary implant to him. David, who was without doubt a capable and progressive cardiologist, accepted the idea.

The next day, on arriving at the selected patient's bed during rounds, the resident announced "Mr. so and so (I don't remember his name) for double mammary implant." Effler, surprised, exclaimed "What?" I explained what I was planning to do. He answered me, smiling: "The red light's going to cause a lot of work tomorrow." Whenever a cardiac arrest occurred, generally in the Intensive Care Unit, a buzzer started to sound and red lights to flash at strategic locations. Every surgeon - understand me well, every one of them -who was not actually engaged in an operation had to run and assist the patient. In general more than one would arrive on the scene, and the first one would have to take charge of the situation. Hence the expression of Effler.

The following day, I dissected the two mammary arteries and implanted the right one in a tunnel parallel to the anterior descending artery and the left one in the lateral wall in a tunnel which coursed below the lateral branches arising from the circumflex artery. That is how in 1966 the double mammary artery implant started. I remember operating on 38 consecutive patients with no mortality, perhaps because we selected each case very carefully.

The only problem to be resolved was that of the residents who had to hold the sternum in a raised position using the normal Farabeuff separators so that the mammaries could be dissected. At the end of the procedure they were exhausted. At the beginning everyone wanted to help, interested in the new operation, but shortly afterwards they would try to escape: either I solved the problem or I would end up without Residents.

What I did was to develop a separator using two vertical bars fixed to the operating table and united by a horizontal bar to which were connected two separators by a special mechanism allowing them to be placed in various positions to maintain the sternum raised and stabilized. This separator, with some modifications we made later, is the one which is used today throughout the world by all the cardiovascular surgical teams involved in the dissection of the mammary arteries and their anastomosis to the coronary tree. This is known as mammary coronary bypass. In addition I developed various instruments to make the tunnels, particularly those in the lateral and diaphragmatic walls, which prevented distortion of the heart during these maneuvers. If the heart is elevated too much, the arterial pressure falls and this can be very dangerous in coronary patients. I always stressed to my assistants that the heart must be treated gently, caressing it as though it were a woman.

When Vineberg learned of the new technique he called us and we arranged for his first visit to our Clinic. During the operation he stood behind me and followed every step with great care while noting down in a little book everything which appeared interesting to him. Afterwards we exchanged views while savoring coffee. The observation which most surprised me was "What large hands you have. At times they did not allow me to see what you were doing." In truth I had never until that moment considered the size of my hands. I remember at one moment going to the bathroom and looking at them through the mirror while washing them, as though they belonged to a stranger.

From then on we became friends. He would visit with us at the Clinic quite often, we would see each other at medical congresses and meetings, and we kept in touch by mail following my return to Buenos Aires until his death on March 26, 1988. He was an innovator who fought tenaciously over many years to get his ideas accepted. Hundreds of patients benefitted from his technique, which was the first to show that deficiency of the coronary circulation could be corrected by surgery.

Effler and Sones were responsible for diffusing the new ideas, principally through conferences and round table discussions. Towards the end of 1966 I decided to analyze the cumulated results of all those patients who had received single or double mammary artery implants. David Fergusson had become an expert in the postoperative study of these patients, particularly those who had received the double implant. In the great majority of cases he could selectively inject either artery using just a single catheter introduced via the right arm. It was in this way that we studied the first patient who had been operated on 10 months previously, and were able to show to our great satisfaction that both mammaries were connected to the majority of the branches of the left coronary.

I wrote a summary and sent it to the committee selecting contributions for the next meeting of the American Association for Thoracic Surgery. Not only was the paper accepted but also was chosen to start the opening session. It was without doubt a great responsibility. Effler revised the final manuscript, despite the editorial help given to me by Mrs. Mildred Hoerr Lysle of the Education Department, in order to be sure that everything was correct. Once the slides were ready, I had to present the paper to the entire group of my colleagues on three occasions with Effler making the pertinent corrections. I was principally worried about my English, for I had decided to memorize the presentation instead of simply reading it. I have always thought that papers which are read from the manuscript are monotonous and at times confusing, it being difficult to synchronize the reading with the order of presentation of the slides.

It is easy to imagine my nervousness and preoccupation as the moment drew near for my participation, the inaugural session being as usual attended by the most distinguished surgeons in our field including some from abroad. Thankfully all went well and Effler closed the discussion with his usual flair. He was more of an orator than a simple speaker. This was to be the first of a long list of presentations over the following years.

The Vineberg operation suffered from the disadvantage that months were necessary for the development of the connections between the implanted artery and the coronary branches. The patient had passed through anesthesia, thoracotomy, dissection of the mammary or mammaries, and tunnelling in his myocardium. He needed time to develop the beneficial effects. If the criteria of selection were met, multiple diffuse lesions with the presence of collaterals and otherwise unaltered myocardium - the morbidity and mortality were low and the results were satisfactory. However, there were cardiologists who continued to challenge the benefits of the procedure despite the cineangiographic evidence and some metabolic studies. They maintained that there was no definitive proof of increased myocardial perfusion, even though undeniable evidence did exist in those patients who were restudied and found to have complete occlusion of the left coronary and whose ventricle received blood only from the mammary implants, and still contracted normally.

I had conclusive but lamentable proof some years later when I reoperated on a patient due to progression of coronary disease. From his first operation he had ample perfusion of the anterior descending territory via an implant of the right mammary artery. On opening the thorax, the saw cut through the artery despite taking the usual extreme care, due to the artery running close under the sternum. A few moments later the electrocardiogram showed significant changes suggesting a large anterior ischemia, the ventricular contraction deteriorated, the heart stopped, and even though we were able to connect the patient to the extracorporeal circulation and perform the programmed bypasses plus an extra one for the descending anterior coronary artery the patient died on the table. The autopsy revealed an extensive anterior infarct. Who could deny the perfusion provided by the internal mammary artery!

The cardiologists referred to us patients who had angina at rest, were incapacitated, and whose cineangiographic studies showed severe narrowing of the initial portions of the coronary arteries, some with lesions of the main left coronary trunk. Faced with the anguish of the families and the demands of the cardiologists who had exhausted all possibilities of medical therapy, we operated knowing the risk we were undertaking. We just did not have a better remedy. Analysis clearly showed that this group of patients suffered a higher mortality and occurrence of postoperative infarcts.

I will always remember one of our patients, a doctor who was a friend of Roy Lewis, the well known cardiologist of our Clinic. He had severe daily pain due to almost total obstruction of the main coronary arteries. As I knew the risk I was taking in operating on him, I moved my hands more rapidly than usual and managed to complete a double mammary artery implant in a little more than one hour. The immediate postoperative period passed without complications, but our colleague died on the third day due to a massive infarct. Without doubt we would have to develop other strategies.

The median anterior incision permitted us for the first time, in 1966, to perform what we called "combined procedures" which were revascularizations (single or double implants) in patients who were suffering from coronary arteriosclerosis who also required valve replacement or repair or even resection of ventricular aneurysm.

Direct repair of coronary obstruction using pericardial or saphenous vein patches in the right coronary artery were relatively frequent (see Figure 7A). The surgical risk was about 10 percent and the long-term evolution satisfactory. When this procedure was done on lesions located in the trunk of the left coronary the mortality was on the contrary extremely high: 11 deaths in 14 patients operated on. Although the repair could be completed in 20 minutes to a half hour, it was done with the aorta completely clamped; as a consequence the heart muscle was not receiving oxygen during this time. At the end of the operation, although the muscle was now abundantly irrigated the damage which had been done at the cellular level was irrecoverable and the contractility of the heart could not be restored. It is easy to understand that a heart which is living with a lesion of the main trunk of the left coronary artery is underperfused and is on the borderline of cellular death from insufficient oxygenation. Any maneuver such as aortic clamping then precipitates death. We tried various modifications. In each case (and I was responsible for most of them) I went to the operating theater feeling a mixture of challenge and fear. The group in charge of renal transplantation, which was a regular procedure in the Cleveland Clinic in those years, did not have sufficient donors. Every time a patient's name appeared on the surgical list with a lesion of the left main coronary trunk, they would be asking for permission to perform a cross-match (tissue typing) with the possible recipients. It was without doubt depressing.

One morning when I was scrubbing up ready to go into the operating theater to face this situation once more, one of the Residents who helped me often and who was a devout Catholic asked me to cease these operations because he felt guilty and indeed had been to church to confess it. I did not give him an answer at that moment but following the surgery, which was one of the few successful cases, I called him into my office and had a long talk with him. I told him that I too was a Catholic, but at the same time I was a surgeon interested in finding a solution to the most serious problem of coronary disease. I had to remind him of the analysis of more than thirteen thousand coronary angiograms made by Proudfit and his colleagues that showed that only 32 patients had survived total occlusion of the main left coronary and that all of these survivors had collaterals arising from the right coronary. I went on to tell him that by having chosen to be a surgeon he had to follow a difficult path full of obstacles and charged with responsibilities towards his patients, whom he must never use as experimental animals but always try to help them in the full knowledge of the risks involved in doing so. I concluded by saying that I did not believe we were making any ethical compromise, and that we were only doing our duty which was sometimes very painful.

It was a custom of the Clinic, without being a written law, that each member of the staff organize a party once a year for all the members of his team. This helped to unify the people and also provided a pleasant and relaxing moment. I had a lot to be thankful for and so Toni and I decided to prepare a typically Argentine barbecue or asado before the end of summer. In my years in Aráuz I had learned how to do it, but the first thing we would need would be to make the asadores which were the crucifix-like frames for spread-eagling the carcasses for cooking in front of the fire, and also the grill itself for cooking other items. I spoke about this with Profeta and with the permission of his chief we made them one Saturday in the basement of the Clinic. It was not a complicated engineering job. The first requirement was a solid vertical bar about six feet in length. About a foot from the top, a series of three holes was drilled at three inch intervals, of sufficient diameter to pass a screw fitted with a wingnut used to fix a two-foot horizontal bar in position. More holes were drilled in the extremes of the horizontal bar to receive wires used to tie the legs of the carcass. Two feet further down the vertical bar, three more holes were drilled but with a bit more space between them than for the upper set, to fix another horizontal bar of equal design. The lower end of the vertical bar was cut to form a spearpoint for inserting into the soil. In this way we constructed the first asadores gauchos in Cleveland. We made four.

On the way to the drilling machine I noticed a roll of stainless steel wire netting, three feet in width and with two-inch spacing between the strands. Perfect for making the grill! Profeta told me that it had been there for some time, left over from a previous job. The foreman told us we could have it with the permission of the chief of the Maintenance Department, which I duly obtained the following Monday. A week later we had a luxury grill, made of nothing less than stainless steel!

Guida, an Argentine who had a delicatessen, pre-pared traditional pork sauages called chorizos and when the time came I went to a slaughterhouse he knew of and selected a complete ribcage, from a prime young animal judging from the size of the ribs and the whiteness of the fat. As an old hand at this business I reckoned it to have been a 400 pound calf. There I met a young Puerto-Rican whom I taught to remove the sweetbreads and other glands which in later asados proved to be the delight of my colleagues.

I also had to find lambs. I had seen sheep on the way to Erie, a city to the northeast of Cleveland, and went there to make sure that two lambs would be ready for the day of the asado. There was no problem, and from then on the farmers of this region became my suppliers. In future asados it was only necessary to call them by phone.

As it was the first asado to be experienced by my guests, I also bought some good-quality steaks.

A few days before the asado, Jack helped me to construct a table of about 15 feet in length. We made it so that the trestles not only supported the planks of the table but also provided support for other planks acting as benches.

Of course, the seating was not sufficient for the 100 or more guests invited, but as usual in a "cookout," they would serve themselves and sit anywhere, usually on the ground in the shade of a tree.

For five dollars we hired the system of coils for cooling beer which permitted us to serve it just like the best German beerhouses. A few bottles of whisky were also made available.

I had piled up more than enough logs, giving myself the luxury of using those from the apple trees which I had cut down. In addition I bought some bags of charcoal for the grill. With Vicente as my assistant, we started very early. Once the asador is put together, the horizontal bars are adjusted to match the size of the animal to be cooked, the latter is then crucified on the asador with the back legs upward. The animal is opened carefully, which occasionally necessitates making small superficial cuts at the union of the ribs with the backbone, inside the carcass, of course. This allows it to be opened like a book and the extremities to be tied with wire using the holes made for this purpose in the ends of the horizontal bars. More lengths of wire are passed through the animal close to the backbone in order to tie on to the vertical bar. The asador is then staked into the ground at an angle of 30 to 45 degrees with the ribs facing the fire. The neck and shoulders must remain about a foot above the ground. If the ground is soft and the asador tends to fall towards the fire, a guy wire is tied to the top of the vertical bar and its other end staked into the ground some six feet back. The same techniques are applied to mount the side of ribs. When a number of asadores are in use, they are arranged in a semicircle around the fire.

The fire itself should be at least four to five feet away from the meat, which cooks very slowly in the radiant heat. When the fire has burned down to embers, these can then be placed closer to the meat and even behind the asadores to provide a uniform heat. Not less than three to four hours are needed for cooking, depending on the size of the animal being selected. Every now and again we sprinkled chimichurri over the meat from a bottle which is closed by a cork with a V-shaped groove cut along its length so that only the liquid emerges. Chimichurri is made from water, salt, pepper, chopped garlic, ground sweetpepper and abundant oregano. It should be made the day before using hot water. When nearly all the guests had arrived we cooked the steaks on the grill, and set out the salads which Toni had prepared.

When the moment finally arrived, each guest was provided with his knife, fork and plate and invited to serve himself with salad and bread. We first served the chorizos which are spiced pork sausages and then the steaks. Then the big moment came when we brought the first lamb. We laid it on a board, untied the wires, and withdrew the asador. The lightly toasted color of the lamb led some to believe that it was not fully cooked. Their minds were soon put at rest when I raised the lamb by its legs and the meat began to separate itself from the bones as I gently shook it. The meat was juicy but showed no sign of being undercooked. Following my advice, most of the guests added a little more chimichurri to their serving and fell to savouring with a will. They confessed that they had never eaten anything as good as this before, even those who normally did not enjoy lamb.

It is well known that the cook does not eat. I was asked when I was going to sample even a little mouthful, but replied with a certain degree of malicious enjoyment, "later, when you have all eaten, I will get some of that cheap meat." I left them to it, and when the majority had finished but were still enjoying the beer, I cut myself a barbecued rib and ate it in the traditional way, slicing it with my knife and serving from knife to mouth. My judgment about the meat was confirmed. It really was from a tender young animal. I slyly asked my guests if they would like to try a little, and despite having eaten their fill they were sufficiently tempted and discovered that this cut of meat when properly cooked is infinitely superior to even the best steak.

I had one more surprise in store. I had asked the Puerto Rican to get some criadillas, which in Argentine restaurants is a euphemism for testicles. I selected the biggest and presented it to Effler telling him it was a good way of building up testosterone. Responding to the general clamor, showing some surprise he gingerly tried it and obviously found it to his liking, for it disappeared in a trice. In the asados that were to follow, usually two per summer, the infamous steaks were left off the menu that returned to the traditional gaucho style. Indeed this proved so popular that the supermarket in Pepper Pike learned how to cut the ribs and offered them packed on trays, not at the same price of course. The meal ended with melons and watermelons and in the afternoon we served coffee with alfajores and palmeritas, which were sweet biscuits made by Toni.

That night, following a healing bath, I felt really satisfied with the asado that had truly expressed our gratitude to all those who had done so much so generously and had made it possible for me to join that big family which is the Cleveland Clinic. Some time later, Crile who was a regular participant in our asados asked me if I would cook for the entire Staff of the Clinic at the annual get-together which instead of being held in a restaurant in the city center would be held at his house in the country. I accepted the challenge and in the Summer of 1970 with the help of his son-in-law, the general surgeon Esselstyn, and using wood which we had cut from dry trees the week before I cooked various lambs and sides of ribs, five hundred and fifty chorizos, and nearly 100 pounds of sweetbreads which the Puerto Rican had gradually accumulated in the freeezer. You might think this exaggerated, but in fact it is just as easy to cook a big asado as it is to cook a small one. It only needs a bit more time in the preparation, and once the asadores are staked in the ground all that is required is to keep an eye on the fire and let the hours pass by. That asado is still remembered in the Clinic (Figure 6).

In addition to my duties in the Department of Thoracic and Cardiovascular Surgery, in 1966 I began to work with Kolff and Nos in the Department of Artificial Organs on the artificial heart project. Some of their grants from the National Institutes of Health required the participation of a cardiovascular surgeon and I was designated for this task. Undoubtedly the project would present a multitude of problems to be resolved, but I dedicated all the time I could to helping out in the operations on calves. We also carried out a number of operations on sheep, replacing mitral valves with aortic valves from the same species.

The cleaning department refused to transport the animal cadavers to the incinerators located in the basement. I never discovered why this was so but suspect that it had a religious basis, for they actively cooperated with us in all other work.

I remember on one occasion in the early evening a sheep in which we had performed a valve transplant died,

Fig. 6. *Argentinian barbecue at Crile's "Knob." Dr. Crile and me.*

and I had to dispose of it. On opening the large oval door of the incinerator, the heat was greater than usual due to the large amount of waste that had been deposited. The sheep was big and heavy, and it took a lot of effort to insert the carcass; part of the hair of my scalp, eyebrows, and arms disappeared in the process.

Today, a number of movements oppose the use of animals in research and to me their arguments are not solidly based. It is certain that an important part of the advance of medicine with its therapeutic implications is due to animal experimentation, without which it is impossible to progress. Perhaps infectious disease constitutes a clear example. What should be controlled is the care of the animals in experimental centers; they should be treated as though they were patients in the hospital.

Perhaps the most far-reaching work we did was a series of lung transplantations in dogs with the help of Paul Taylor, who was a Resident in our department. We had acquired a lot of experience in routine lung resections and this contributed to our experimental work. We had only two failures in bronchial anastomoses, which was the most common complication reported in the literature, perhaps because we used interrupted sutures. Despite the few drugs available to combat rejection, some of these dogs survived for as long as 3 months, and Fergusson had the chance of performing catheterizations which showed that the peripheral part of the lungs was not adequately perfused.

I remember going to the annual meeting of the American College of Surgeons in Chicago in October, where Lower and Shumway presented their results on heart transplantation in dogs. The lecture finished with a color movie showing a bitch playing with her puppies. Lower told us that she was a transplantation animal and had gone through her pregnancy with no problems. This caused a stir in the audience, and when the noise died down he then told us that the father too was a transplantation animal! On my way home I asked myself "Why are they waiting to do this in humans? the techniques are fully developed." A short time later Barnard proved me right.

My friendship with Kolff deepened as a result of working in his Department, and has been one of the greatest satisfactions my profession has given me. He deserves enormous respect for his contributions which include the development of the artificial kidney, but I admire him most for being an exceptional humanist who continues to live a simple life and above all gives the greatest importance to spiritual values.

Meanwhile, we continued our intensive surgical work. We had developed the patch technique to the point of using it in more extensive lesions particularly in the right coronary artery where the repair was sometimes several centimeters long. We soon discovered that a number of these repairs thrombosed and occluded the artery. The longer the repair the more likely it was to thrombose because we left the often irregular internal wall intact. These irregularities produced turbulence that encouraged clot formation.

3

The Aortocoronary Bypass

At the beginning of 1967 I began to think about the possibility of using the saphenous vein in coronary surgery. The Cleveland Clinic had accumulated a lot of experience in the use of the vein in patients with occlusion of the circulation in the lower limbs and also in the renal arteries in hypertensives. I asked myself: why not in the coronaries? I mentioned the idea to Mason and after thinking about it for some time I concluded that the ideal patient would have the right coronary artery occluded in its upper third but with good angiographic visualization of the vessel beyond the obstruction via collaterals arising from the left coronary. If for any reason the vein became occluded, nothing would happen and the patient would revert anatomically to his previous state.

The first operation was done in May 1967 on a 57-year-old male patient who had been studied by David Fergusson. I vividly remember that we performed the operation in Room 17. After connecting the patient to the heart-lung machine, we placed a small clamp almost at the origin of the right coronary artery and we exposed its lumen (the channel through which the blood flows) and prepared it for the anastomosis (connection), transecting the artery diagonally at an angle of about 45 degrees to increase the effective size of the artery and to prevent possible subsequent narrowing. We obtained a length of vein from the upper thigh and made the anastomosis using 6-0 silk interrupted sutures, that is to say with a very delicate sized needle. On releasing the proximal clamp, the blood flowed rapidly from the open end. The clamp was reapplied. We then prepared the distal (further out) segment and repeated the anastomosis (Figure 7B). We released the distal clamp previously applied tying the last sutures to displace any possible air bubbles. On freeing the clamp near the origin of the artery, we could see the branches of the right coronary fill with blood.

The postoperative period was normal and understandably Mason was anxious to restudy the patient. I personally wanted to wait a few days more but on the eighth day he repeated the catheterization. He called me immediately, but I had to finish the operation I was doing at the time. On my arrival at B10 he showed me the movie he had obtained. The right coronary had been completely reconstructed, the anastomoses were barely visible and showed no narrowing, and the filling of the artery beyond the graft was excellent. I had rarely seen Mason so excited. He could not stop waving his arms about and congratulating me. A few days later he went to Germany to participate in a congress and took a copy of the film with him. Technically, the interposition of a length of saphenous vein had its limitations and we soon began to anastomose the proximal part of the vein to the front wall of the ascending aorta, starting in operation number 15. This was achieved by partial clamping of the aorta to isolate a segment of the wall where we made a small hole and used 6-0 or 5-0 interrupted silk sutures to anastomose the vein to the aorta, generally after having connected the vein to the right coronary beyond the occlusion (Figure 7C). In this way we "bypassed" the occlusion, hence the name of the operation. In Spanish the equivalent is called "bridging" the occlusion.

At the beginning the patients were very carefully selected due to the lack of any previous experience. Sones once more showed his profound respect for the patient, advising me: "René, be cautious. We must wait until we can show that they do not obstruct." I was convinced that they would last, being connected directly to the origin of the aorta just like a natural coronary and receiving a vigorous expan-

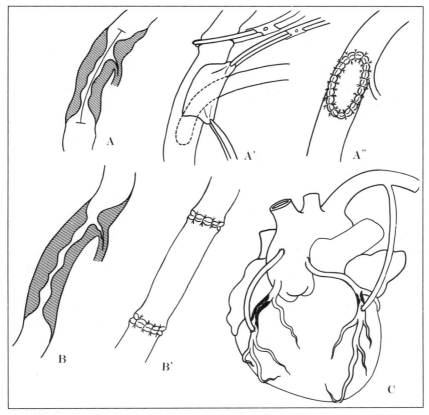

Fig. 7. *The evolution of direct coronary surgery. A: 1962: The patch graft technique. B: 1967: The interposed saphenous vein graft technique. C: 1967: On the left, saphenous vein graft bypass. 1970: On the right, left internal mammary artery bypass graft.*

sion every time the heart beat. It was however logical and humane not to rush ahead.

Some might ask why we went ahead with the bypass technique without first perfoming animal experiments. Were we not risking a case of malpractice? It is evident that in medicine animal experimentation is of great importace but it is not always obligatory. In our own case the bypass resulted from intensive work on hundreds of patients affected by coronary disease and meticulous analysis of every patient. We always carefully informed the patient and his family before trying anything new, and always required his consent.

We did not think about a malpractice suit, which in those days was not too common. These days it is all too frequent and there now exists a real industry complete with specialized lawyers and doctors who are prepared to testify against their own colleagues for large sums of money. Malpractice suits generally have lamentable consequences for our profession. First because they retard medical progress and act against the patient's interest by not permitting the doctor to make an appropriate decision due to fear of a lawsuit, and second because they significantly increase the cost of medical care. A few examples should suffice. I was once on a visit to Spokane where a young surgeon was performing an aortic valve replacement. The root of the aorta and the valve ring proved to be small, and the correct decision was substitution with a mechanical valve. When the moment arrived he asked the nurse for such a valve, and she responded that the patient had asked for a biological valve and that this figured in his case history:

"Doctor, the patient signed for a biological valve. It is my duty to emphasize this. If you use a mechanical valve you do so at your own risk."

Faced with this dilemma, the young surgeon asked me:

"What would Dr. Favaloro do?"

I answered:

"The best for the patient. You know very well that biological valves have base rings that are too wide and the use of one in this case would only be a partial solution."

He thought about it for a few minutes and then used the mechanical valve. I do not know what happened when the patient got to know about it.

Another example: a person receives a knock on the head as a result of an accident, experiencing nothing more than transient dizziness. The correct thing to do is to place him under observation for 24 or 48 hours and monitor his evolution. Fear of a malpractice suit however leads to him being sent for a whole battery of tests including computerized tomography or even nuclear magnetic resonance, both being highly expensive studies.

A patient might enter the emergency room with all the symptoms of acute gastritis. He will be submitted to radiography and exhaustive analysis with endoscopes. "I don't want him to worsen and have a lawsuit later" is the argument used by many. The profession is haunted by the spectre of malpractice always at our side. Surgeons in particular must pay large sums of money to the insurance companies for protection.

The worst example I know of was told to me by one of Sones' former Residents. He had made a catheterization study using puncture of the right femoral artery at the level of the groin with no problem. Two months later he was accused by the patient who professed that since the study he had become impotent. His pulses were normal and there could be no connection whatsoever between the study and his sexual misadventures. To settle out of court cost the doctor 90 thousand dollars.

In the Cleveland Clinic we were protected by the Institution. I personally had two cases. The first was an accusation made by a colleague two years after I had performed a valve replacement on him. He had received dental treatment which resulted in an infection, bacterial endocarditis, which finally localized in the valve which then required reoperation. His argument was that I had not told him that prosthetic heart valves could become infected. He said that he would have reconsidered the operation if he had been informed of this possibility at the time. I sent him a long letter in which I asked him to remember the circumstances of his admission to the Clinic with advanced heart failure, in addition to other considerations of which he should have been aware as a medical man. The second case was brought by the relatives of an old Hungarian lady who came to our service suffering from a massive tumor occupying a large part of her right lung. In the morning I made a routine bronchoscopic examination and obtained samples of secretions from the most distant parts of the bronchial tree using a fine catheter carrying a tiny piece of gauze at its tip. These samples would be sent for histological examination to determine if the tumor was a cancer. In the Intensive Care Unit she began to bleed a lot and this provoked coughing of sufficient intensity to make her short of breath. With the agreement of her family we performed an emergency operation and made a total resection of her right lung. The pathological anatomy study revealed the tumor to be benign, anthracosis, but highly invasive having involved the bronchial wall. This meant that rubbing the wall during the bronchoscopy provoked the bleeding. Her postoperative course was normal but on the ninth day she died suddenly when getting up in the morning to go to the bathroom. Her relatives refused to let us perform an autopsy, and I was called to court. The lawyer acting for the family was a well-known practitioner of this type of lawsuit. His turn came to interrogate me.

"You are Argentine, right?"

"Yes, of course."

"You did your general surgery training in your own country, right?"

"Yes, of course."

"Your honor - he continued - we all know that the teaching of general surgery in Argentina cannot be compared with ours because of its inferior quality."

I began to get nervous.

"You don't have your Board in general Surgery, isn't that right?"

"That is right."

"You received your training in thoracic and cardio-vascular surgery in the Cleveland Clinic, but you do not have your Board exam in that either, isn't that right?"

"That is right."

"As you can see we are confronted with two big problems - he continued - which start with his deficient training in Argentina."

This was insupportable. I quickly rose to my feet and said:

"Your honor, we are in front of a lawyer who is a son of a bitch," (I had adopted some extramedical traits of Mason).

"Take a note of that!"

"Take two notes of it! I exclaimed."

I asked not to be interrupted. I told them how I had been accepted as a member of the American College of Surgeons and the American Association for Thoracic Surgery despite not having the respective Boards, because both Societies considered that I should be admitted on the basis of my contributions even though this did not fully comply with the rules, that my case records in the Cleveland Clinic included hundreds of bronchoscopies without any accidents, that the operation would have had to have been done anyway, that the postoperative period was uncomplicated, that the death had occurred on the day the patient was to be discharged from the Clinic, and that in any case we would never know the true cause of death because the autopsy had been refused. Despite all this, the Clinic had to settle out of court. I do not know for how much money.

Malpractice suits are in my opinion unjustified in the majority of cases and are only to the detriment of our profession. I believe that the only solution is that the practitioner who has been found not guilty should immediately sue the petitioner for damages. In this way the lawyers working in this industry would think twice about starting a lawsuit.

Our workload was forever increasing and the facilities of the second floor were just not sufficient. The waiting list grew longer and it became common for patients to wait between two and three months for surgery.

The sixth floor was completely occupied by the Obstetrics Department which, although a busy department, was not one of great importance to the Clinic. With a minimum of changes it could easily be converted into an efficient Department of Cardiovascular Surgery. The delivery rooms could be transformed into operating rooms and the immediate postpartum rooms into postoperative recovery rooms. The idea grew, and we analyzed it with Effler on various occasions before it was finally considered by the Board of Governors and the Board of Trustees. The members of this latter board, which was concerned mainly with institutional politics and changes, called me to a meeting and subjected me to a detailed interrogation. Their main interest was whether we could keep all the beds occupied in a unit that would be a first in our area. I replied that not only would we fill the beds but would be asking for even more room considering the high incidence and high risk of coronary disease. Only in this way could we begin to approach it from a solid basis. The Board finally resolved that there would be no more deliveries in the Cleveland Clinic.

My part in the development of the Department of Cardiovascular Surgery was especially concerned with the operative area. I was principally worried about the time lost between operations. Three operating rooms were projected, one anesthesia induction room, and one large room for surgical supplies where the operating tables could be set up with their instruments. Towards the back, between the operating rooms, was a space for rapid sterilization using new equipment which could do the job in only a few minutes. At the entrance, to the left, was a room for all the members of the group without discrimination: staff, residents, scrub nurses, general nurses and technicians all together in the brief moments of rest. In this way we brought to an end the separation of groups which existed on the second floor. I have always believed that persons in the surgical area should act together as a family, from the surgeon to the cleaner, to obtain the best results. I do not tire of repeating that the only person to receive privileges is the patient. The act of being together sharing a cup of tea or coffee, exchanging ideas and commenting on the events of the day is highly beneficial and helps to build the spirit of solidarity so vital in cardiovascular surgery, particularly in difficult situations - emergencies or complications - when differences of rank disappear.

This organization permitted three patients to occupy the operating rooms in the morning. When an operation was drawing to a close, the next patient was anesthetized in the induction room, arterial and venous lines were placed for monitoring, as were the cables for the electrocardiogram and rectal and esophageal thermometers. The patient was then ready for the operation. To expedite even more, we fitted wheels to the operating tables so that the patient entered and left the operating room without the need to transfer him from one table to another.

The system worked as follows: at the end of the first operation the patient left the operating room on the operating table; the operating room was cleaned in a few minutes: the next patient, already anesthetized, was then wheeled in, followed by the table carrying the instruments and which had a special double sterile drape. The table was positioned over the lower part of the patient's body leaving thorax, abdomen and thighs in view. Meanwhile the surgical team including the scrub nurse was ready to begin. The nurse's assistant removed the first sterile drape and the scrub nurse entered into action. In a few minutes the drapes were in position and the operative field was ready. For the head end of the operating table I had designed a device which was mounted on four vertical bars fixed to the operating table and fitted with a shelf on which some instruments could be placed to make the scrub nurse's job easier. This device left the patient's head and neck in view for the anesthetist to work freely while isolating this area from that of the surgeon. A secondary advantage was that of maintaining the spectators at a prudent distance. Bottles and bags of blood and other fluids could be conveniently hung from both ends of the structure. The "monster," as it was christened was and still is of great utility, most visiting surgeons have made detailed sketches of it and taken measurements to construct it in their own institutions, since it is not commercially available. I have never patented any of my instruments, not even the separator used for dissection of the mammary arteries of which over 200 thousand have been sold. All of these ideas and developments helped to reduce the time between operations to 20 to 30 minutes. This degree of organization never ceased to impress the many surgeons who came to visit us. With three operating rooms in use we could regularly operate on ten patients per day.

I believe that the relationship between the medical profession and industries directly related to our field has spawned danger. With declining government funds for scientific and technological development, professionals and medical institutions must resort to the private sector which involves a risk: the physician investigator may be transformed into an advertiser (receiving significant economic benefits of course) for this or that drug or new technology, with results being distorted and statistical data being altered.

This is not a product of my imagination; it can be seen in published papers and at important scientific meetings. Fortunately this has brought a beneficial reaction, and prestigious physicians have written editorials about the problem, which has also been discussed at round-table sessions.

I believe it is necessary to establish rigid ethical guidelines. We need the cooperation of private organizations to continue our teaching and research activities, but this should not involve any compromises. If a new drug or technology is being tested, the final analysis should be undertaken by a third party and the initial publications should not include the names of the professionals involved in the trial. The editors of important medical journals have an enormous responsibility today, and with their advisory staff must be more watchful than ever when reviewing papers submitted for publication.

To give an idea of what can happen, I remember the opening conference a few years ago of the American College of Cardiology annual meeting. This was dedicated to a new thrombolytic (a substance that destroys blood clots) for use in the acute stage of a myocardial infarct. I knew the subject well, it being one of my great interests since 1968. I waited and waited for the speaker, a distinguished cardiologist, to refer to the complications of the treatment, which had some worrisome aspects, and not just to the benefits. The talk closed with great praise for the new drug, which cost $2,000 dollars per patient. The following morning I had a working breakfast with an important person from NIH who had arrived the night before. When he asked me for news of the meeting, I told him what had happened in the opening conference. He quickly replied: "What you don't know René, is that the company presented him with $900,000 dollars in stocks."

Returning to our construction of the surgical suite, having the intensive care room almost next door was an enormous advantage. The rest of the floor was occupied by preoperative and postoperative patients. It was no longer necessary to walk all over the hospital to see our patients, except for those with thoracic disease who were still operated on on the second floor. The organization worked perfectly and significantly reduced complications and deaths.

The year 1968 saw great developments in aortocoronary bypass. Following the lines we had developed in 1966 we could operate on patients with ventricular aneurysm or valvular disease and at the same time repair their coronaries, due to the routine use of coronary cineangiography in all patients with valvular disease whether or not they had experienced angina. We were surprised to find patients who did not have angina often had severe coronary lesions. This cautious attitude was based on prior sad experiences. For example I had operated on a 52-year-old man, from Pittsburgh, who had a severely calcified aortic valve. His postoperative period was normal and he was discharged after ten days. A week later he died suddenly and autopsy, which is frequently performed in the U.S., demonstrated coronary disease and death due to a clot in the middle third of an enormous right coronary which had led to a massive infarct. Little by little we learned that patients without symptoms could have coronary disease, and so began to make routine use of coronary cineangiography in all cases of valvular disease.

In Buenos Aires we have continued clinical investigation of this important aspect of coronary disease. If a patient has presenting symptoms of carotid disease, aneurysm of the abdominal aorta, or obstruction of the arteries of the lower extremities we perform coronary cineangiography in addition to angiography of the region which is the objective of the consultation, even if the patient does not have coronary symptoms; this procedure does not increase the risk to the patient. In this way we demonstrate that a significant number of patients have severe coronary lesions including those of the left main trunk. With absolute responsibility we first revascularize the coronaries and then some days or weeks later operate for the original disease, except in the case of the carotids which may be operated on with the coronary arteries at the same time.

Results demonstrate that deaths and complications particularly in operations for abdominal aortic aneurysm are significantly decreased. Also we have found that in young patients with previous infarct but now recuperated and symptomless, coronary cineangiography reveals that a third of them have diffuse lesions. Our knowledge of the natural history of coronary disease justifies surgery in selected cases following careful analysis of the angiographic results. We believe that this approach is amply justified in view of the information already presented in the introduction. Silent ischemia is a term referring to patients who have insufficient circulation despite their being asymptomatic. This is a condition under continuous study. Non-invasive methods, from the common stress test (ergometry) up to a PET scan, are helping to clarify this problem and its therapeutic indications.

Also in 1968 we began to perform bypasses of the left coronary. One of the first cases was the "test case" of a patient with a severe lesion of the main trunk of the artery and minimal alteration of its branches. A simple bypass anastomosing the anterior descending artery at its most proximal portion led to filling of the entire left coronary bed, confirmed by the postoperative study. At last the most formidable lesion to be encountered in coronary pathology had been beaten! This was without a doubt one of the greatest satisfactions in my life as a cardiovascular surgeon. How we had suffered before!

For a long time I had thought that patients could benefit from rapid restoration of oxygenated blood to the heart muscle during the first moments of an acute infarct, and also in the case of recurrent angina at rest with documented electrocardiographic changes during the periods of pain.

This arose from my own observations. When a patient died, I always tried to be present at the autopsy and at times performed it myself. Dr. Larry McCormack was in charge of the cardiovascular section of the Pathology Department and he cooperated in this by waiting at times until I had finished my work in the operating room. As I have already commented, the patients who received a Vineberg operation for left main coronary disease had a high mortality. When they died, which was generally a sudden death over a few minutes, clinical and electrocardiographic observation indicated that the principal cause was acute infarction. This could not be confirmed on careful examination of the heart or by use of the common histologic techniques. Mac (as we called McCormack) used to say to me "he died too suddenly." For me it was difficult to understand how the clinical and electrocardiographic signs indicated infarct whereas the pathologic anatomy of cells from the area of this "infarct" showed only slight changes. The publications on experimental work, especially one by Cox and his colleagues, showed that in the first hours of an infarct the majority of the heart muscle was not in fact dead. I thought that if fresh oxygenated blood could be brought to these cells in time, the damage could be prevented or minimized. Could the bypass technique achieve it?

Despite the new facilities, we continued to have a waiting list for the sixth floor. Those patients with especially critical obstructive lesions were lodged generally in the Bolton Square Hotel and were operated on as soon as possible.

I usually got to the Clinic at 7 a.m. One day in April 1968 the Resident on call told me that one of the patients had experienced severe pain at 6 a.m. and was in poor condition. This patient's previous coronary arteriogram had shown a severe lesion near the beginning of his long anterior descending artery. We went to his room and found him to be cold and sweating, slightly cyanotic - that is to say his skin was blue denoting inadequate oxygenation of the blood - and breathing rapidly and with difficulty. His arterial pressure was low. Given his case history, we were certain that he was experiencing an acute infarction which was confirmed by the electrocardiogram.

While the patient was on his way to the coronary unit, I went to B10. Fortunately, Sones had arrived by then and I discussed with him the possibility of performing an emergency operation, because the patient had been referred to him for coronary cineangiography. As always, his love and respect for his patients caused him to raise some objections which I refuted, telling him of my own observations and reviewing the published experimental work. My enthusiasm proved to be stronger than his objections and he accepted. Both of us knew from the angiographic findings that the patient was close to death and that if he did survive his heart muscle could remain severely damaged due to the sheer size of his anterior descending territory. This meant that he might be incapacitated for life.

When the patient had been transferred to the sixth floor I explained the situation to his family who accepted the decision to operate. As in so many emergencies, the whole team moved quickly. Viljoen anesthetized him in seconds after administering small doses of medication to maintain the blood pressure, and we had him on extracorporeal circulation in a few minutes. On opening the pericardium we could see that the front and side walls of the left ventricle did not contract; the ventricle appeared to be distended and somewhat cyanotic. It was necessary to decompress the heart as soon and as much as possible, so we gently placed a medium-sized catheter into the left ventricle by way of the right upper pulmonary vein and continuously aspirated the arriving blood. It is well known that if the pressure within the left ventricular cavity increases significantly the coronary circulation is compromised even if the coronaries are normal. This is especially true for the coronaries perfusing the deeper layers of the heart muscle. It was for this reason that we had to decompress the left ventricle throughout the operation.

In the light of past experience we made a bypass from the aorta to the anterior descending artery, and we could see how the wall of the left ventricle gradually recovered its color and contractility. We kept the patient on extracorporeal circulation and with his ventricle being decompressed for half an hour more. His heart began to contract more vigorously and we gradually reduced the flow from the pump until his ventricle was maintaining the entire flow by itself. The blood pressure showed constant improvement and it was not necessary to administer medication. On the following day the patient whose functions we had been monitoring continuously, was extubated - that is to say disconnected from the respirator - and continued his recuperation without any problems. The electrocardiogram showed only a minimal alteration in the anterior wall. When I entered his office to give him the good news, Mason exclaimed "René, another first!" And indeed it was. The bypass technique had been employed for the first time in a patient suffering an acute infarct.

The cineangiographic study made ten days later showed the only damage to be restricted to a zone of slightly reduced contractility about half an inch in diameter located in the center of the anterior wall. The rest contracted normally. Our first publication summarized the results of 18 patients with preinfarction angina and 11 patients with acute infarction. In the conclusion I wrote: "When the operation is carried out within the first six hours following an acute myocardial infarction, most of the myocardium can be saved. Cardiovascular surgeons can now adopt a more aggressive attitude in the surgical treatment of patients with acute coronary insufficiency." Even now when it is accepted without discussion that the first six hours are of fundamental importance I am still surprised by the fact that these still relevant conclusions were based on only 11 patients with acute infarct.

Years later the Spokane group proved in a large series of patients that successful surgical treatment of acute infarction is possible. More recently the fibrinolytics - drugs which dissolve blood clots - in combination with angioplasty and coronary surgery have saved many lives.

Nowadays it is universally accepted that an infarct is the consequence of interruption of blood flow through one of the branches of the coronary arteries due to blockage by a thrombus (blood clot). The segment of muscle supplied by this branch then dies. The size of the infarct depends on the size of the coronary branch, but as we have already observed, the muscle does not die immediately and if blood flow is restored in time some or all of the muscle can recover.

The fibrinolytics act by dissolving the clot and can reestablish the circulation in most patients if given quickly, within the first three hours if at all possible. Where do these clots come from? The answer is well known. Arteriosclerosis produces plaques of different shapes and sizes in the walls of the coronary arteries, and the rupture of a plaque produces a tear in the thin layer of the artery (the intima) in contact with the blood. This unleashes a complex process whose final result is the formation of a clot. As we can see, the atheromatous plaque has a fundamental role in this process and will continue to do so even after the thrombus has dissolved, its size being of great importance. If the plaque obstructs only 20 percent of the vessel diameter after the clot disappears the patient will almost certainly recover and the intimal tear will scar over. In contrast if the plaque is large enough to interfere with blood flow through the artery even after the clot has gone, a new thrombus may form or scar tissue worsens the degree of obstruction. This is serious when the diameter is reduced by 70 percent or more. Under these circumstances, angioplasty (balloon dilatation) or coronary surgery are necessary to avoid grave consequences. I believe that we must not have a false sense of security when the clinical evolution indicates that all is well, especially in the case of young patients. The use of coronary cineangiography, preceded or not by functional tests, is mandatory in determining the correct course to follow.

In the same year, March 1968, I made a double reconstruction using the technique of interposition, and in December we performed a double bypass of the right coronary and anterior descending arteries. In this way we opened the doors to multiple bypasses in which the contributions of Dudley Johnson and his colleagues in Milwaukee were of real importance.

It was evident that in those patients with multiple lesions one or two bypasses could not solve the whole problem because the different sites along the coronary tree were not interconnected. Hence the need to increase the number of bypasses. In general the patients with multiple lesions benefitted from three or four and exceptionally five bypasses. In very special circumstances we can remember having made six. The number of bypasses to be made must be carefully determined by analysis of the coronary cineangiogram and not in the operating room by examination and palpation of the coronary arteries as we have seen on visits to some cardiovascular surgery centers. The reputation of the surgeon is not based on the number of bypasses he can perform but on the judgment he exercises in the preoperative analysis of the coronary cineangiogram and on the surgical results. Patients must understand that a larger number of bypasses does not signify better protection. Unfortunately we will never be able to exclude from the profession those who, as in any field of surgery, strut like peacocks and confess their "pride" in having made "nine bypasses" only to be contested by "I made eleven," without realizing that they have demonstrated nothing by this except their deficient personalities. Poor patients who fall into their hands!

In a paper which was accepted for publication in the *Journal of Thoracic and Cardiovascular Surgery* in December 1968 I summarized everything we had learned until then about the aortocoronary bypass technique. We had operated on 171 patients, the largest series in the world. In the paper I demonstrated how we had advanced carefully, analyzing every single case in detail to avoid committing errors in selecting the patients from the large number studied every day by Sones and colleagues at B10.

During that year and the following one the number of visitors anxious to see our work increased considerably, as did my participation in meetings and congresses in the U.S. and outside, especially in Europe and Latin America. To ease these tasks I enlisted the help of the Eduction Department, principally the photographic, movie and medical art sections, in the preparation of excellent teaching material which in addition to slides included movies of the preoperative studies, color shots of the most important phases of the operations, and the postoperative studies. I remember that after finishing my day's work I would go down to B10 where I spent hours editing the coronary angiographic studies on an old viewer which permitted me to wind and rewind by hand, eliminating the unwanted footage and gluing together the strips which were important. The final result was of real value in discussion and analysis with my colleagues.

I also prepared posters for presentation at the annual meetings of the American Heart Association and the American College of Cardiology. For this latter society a large poster was prepared, including replicas made by a sculptor of the most frequently employed bypasses; it was awarded a prize. These medical meetings occasionally produced a sour taste because it was difficult to convince the cardiologists in spite of the evidence available. I well remember when Mason and I were invited to a prestigious university in the South of the United States. Once our presentations had been completed, the customary discussion session became hotter and hotter until someone said that our attitude to the patients was totally dehumanizing. Mason lost his temper and it would be unwise to reproduce here the epithets which flew through the air. Those who knew Sones only through his participation in meetings, where he was generally aggressive and even disrespectful, will never appreciate that he was an extremely sensitive person who enjoyed but also suffered with his patients, whom he loved deeply. His passionate struggle to impose the technique of coronary cineangiography led him to get Earl Shirey, his close collaborator, to catheterize him. Who else could he have chosen? Earl was a wise physician who could also push a catheter like no other, with unusual dexterity and above all mature judgment during the maneuvers. The catheterization showed normal coronaries and Mason would occasionally show his films during meetings to emphasize the low risk of the procedure.

He always wanted me to call him as soon as possible after each operation to inform him of the details, as though his life depended on the results. I have been witness to his tears when we were defeated and at times he disappeared from B10 until the following day. The same happened if something went wrong during a catheterization. The real physician suffers when things go wrong, especially the surgeon. If a patient dies after an operation, the relationship between death and the surgeon is usually much more direct than in the case of a physician. After having exercised my profession for more than 40 years, the loss of a patient still affects me as much as it did the first time. I still cannot get used to it; my colleagues know this and are witnesses in the operating room when I fight and fight to save the patient even when all the evidence indicates that further attempts will be useless. Death is my principal enemy but knows that he must wait until I am absolutely exhausted before he can take one of my patients. If ever the day arrives on which I stop suffering, I will take it as a sign that the scalpel should be taken from my hands.

Mason sacrificed everything to his profession, he burned his eyes and had to be operated on for cataracts as a result of too much radiation. His first marriage was destroyed. He lived in B10 and for B10; it was his true home. As a pioneer he was ahead of his time and had to fight to impose his ideas, sometimes at a disadvantage, because his discoveries brought to an end many myths defended by eminent cardiologists who, despite the evidence, continued standing on their false pedestals, and reacting violently. I tried always to sit by his side when we participated together in a discussion and when I could see him about to explode I would put a hand on his knee and press strongly to make him calm down.

The medical meetings fortunately did not always finish in arguments and misunderstandings, and I well remember pleasant meetings, especially when we were invited to smaller centers or hospitals at the community level.

There are so many anecdotes about our time together. We once went to La Crosse, Wisconsin, to an important local Clinic to present our work. We traveled in an old airplane which stopped in various places before arriving at La Crosse. The trip was made early in the morning without any trouble. We arrived at the hospital and presented our studies to the pleasure of all in a spirit of comradeship, and we even examined some patients. The return flight was due to leave at 8 p.m. so we ate simply with some drinks imbibed by Mason as was his custom. When we were on the way to the airport a great storm blew in from the West. It started to rain shortly before takeoff and the little airplane began to dance around in the air until it managed to outrun the storm and land at the next stop. There the sequence was repeated, the storm having caught up with us and for the first part of the next leg the plane was thrown around like a leaf torn from a tree and ready to be dashed into the ground at any moment.

During each leg of the flight Sones would ask for a "double Scotch" and talked continuously; "René, I think this is a plane which was in the second world war. I don't believe it can resist much longer. I am sorry for you, my death is of no importance but you still have much to achieve." As you can imagine this cheered me up a lot.

Believe it or not, during part of the flight, drops of water fell from the ceiling of the plane as a result of flying almost all the time in the midst of the storm. Our next stop was Milwaukee and there it was announced that the Chicago airport was closed. I was not prepared to go on. Despite all Mason was happy, thanks to the whiskey. I called the nearest hotel, reserved a room, and arranged for a limousine to be sent to the airport. Due to the rain we waited inside near the door. The limousine arrived, failed to see us, and went on its way. Mason proposed that we start walking. Far away we could see the lights of the city, but to him they appeared closer. I could not convince him. As we were travelling with nothing more than briefcases, he picked up his and began to walk. A few minutes later we found ourselves walking in the dark along the highway and thumbing every car which passed by, hoping that someone would take pity on us. By sheer good luck we had covered only a mile before someone stopped and took us to the hotel.

Early the following morning there was a direct flight to Cleveland. I made the reservations and called the Clinic to delay my operations and Mason's catheterizations for a few hours. Mason was now in profound sleep. I called the desk and asked for us to be awakened in sufficient time to eat breakfast and travel to the airport. When we were up I made him look out of the window so that he could see really how far we were from the airport.

On another occasion we went to St. Joseph's Hospital in New Jersey at the invitation of Brocato, a highly respected cardiologist in that area. The meeting was arranged for Saturday morning so we arrived on Friday night. During the evening meal my attention was called to the fact that a large number of the doctors bore Italian names. Next day the session began as always with Mason talking about coronary cineangiography followed by my presentation of our surgical experience. When my turn came, the doctor making the introduction emphasized that I came from South America and more precisely from Argentina. Before entering into my specific theme I mentioned my surprise at hearing so many Italian names and said that this made me feel quite at home because the majority of the population of my country was also of Italian origin and in my particular case Sicilian. More than applause this comment provoked an explosion, and I could hear cries of Bravo! Bravo! I finished my talk in the midst of applause and the majority of those present shook my hand, some slapping my back heartily. I did not understand this reaction at all. We lunched and went straight to the airport. In the plane I asked Mason the reasons for such a display. He answered me with a smile "You good old son of a bitch," which was one of his more common expressions but said without the specific sense of the words used. "Didn't you know that New Jersey is one of the most important centers of the Mafia?"

The result of this trip was that from that day on Mason studied and I operated on a large number of patients from New Jersey, some of them important Mafiosi. We discovered that Cleveland also had its connections, some of whom passed through our hands. I even operated on the Godfather of the Southeastern United States who lived at that time in Georgia, and some others from Las Vegas. It was almost always necessary to reserve a number of rooms for them, for they were accompanied by members of their families and by their ubiquitous bodyguards. One of these Mafiosi asked me when I visited him the day before his operation if his bodyguard could be present in the theater during the operation. I jumped to my feet and told him "Get yourself another surgeon. You do not have any confidence in me. You have also insulted me. You forget that I too have Sicilian blood" and left the room. A short time later some members of his family came to see me, I went back to the room and he apologized profusely with tears in his eyes. I operated on him the next day and fortunately he recovered well with no complications.

The trip I will never forget as long as I live was in Summer of 1969. We took our wives, Mason having remarried, and toured the south of France, Italy, and Spain. We flew first to Marseilles where Professor De Vernejoul acted as the honorary president of a congress attended by representatives of most of the European countries including some from the Eastern block. In addition to the medical interchange he had organized social gatherings which were very enjoyable.

Besides savouring freshly caught fish in the bayside restaurants, we were taken one night to dine in a medieval castle outside the city. The first dish was a paté. Professor De Vernejoul sat next to me and explained that in the center of the paté was a specially cooked small bird which according to him was a culinary delight. In truth it was there and still with its head in place. I looked at the wives of my foreign medical colleagues and especially at mine. The majority, on discovering the bird, stopped eating including Toni, who later told me she had almost vomited. All in all it was only part of the refined French school of cooking and was indeed truly enjoyable.

During the meal, Professor De Vernejoul occasionally wrote notes on some small sheets of paper at hand. During dessert, he gave an improvised speech which I shall never forget. The participants in the meeting in Marseilles had come from all over Europe, including the east. To these colleagues, some very distinguished, he named country by country and spoke a little about the characteristics of each one of them and referred to their important historical events. He surely had jotted all this down on his notes. De Vernejoul was without doubt one of the most qualified representatives of French culture.

Our next meeting was to be in Verona after the weekend and I proposed that we travel by car. At first Sones and his wife Phyllis were reluctant but finally accepted. I rented a spacious station wagon and we drove along the coast. We left early on Saturday morning. We had arranged to lunch and rest for a short while in a seaside house owned by Sisteron, a surgeon from Lyon, about 200 kilometers from Marseilles. Mason was very happy. Everything caught his attention. During the afternoon, for example, we stopped on a deserted slope above the sea and ran down to the water where Mason took off his shoes and socks, rolled up his trouser legs and jumped and ran at the water's edge just like a child.

We spent the night in a small hotel and resumed our trip early in the morning, arriving in Milan before noon. We paid a quick visit to the cathedral and then went on, using secondary roads which ran through the Tuscan country-side. I realized very quickly that this giant of modern cardiology knew very little about nature. He had spent so long shut up in his laboratory or flying in airplanes that everything he saw impressed him. I had to stop at frequent intervals:

"Look! A wheat field, almost ripe, look how beautiful! The ears are dancing in the wind! Look at the red wild poppies!"

And I would stop, get out of the car to gather stems of wheat and flowers and put them into his hands.

"Look! look at those vines!"

And stop to gather grapes for him to taste.

"Look! that is a fig tree. The last figs of summer are so sweet." " They are always like that, Mason; you can eat them without peeling them if you wish. Look at those tomatoes! those eggplants, that lettuce!"

This ceremony repeated itself an infinite number of times.

In a bend in the road near a house there was a peach tree laden with yellow fruit blushing red. I felt obliged to ask the owners to sell me some rather than just pick them off the tree uninvited. On discovering that we came from the United States and making friends with my poor Italian, they insisted on us getting out of the car and, together with the peaches, they served us their home made red wine. I asked for a knife and peeled and chopped the peaches, adding them to the wine just as my grandfather had done when I was a child. We waited a few minutes before tasting, and Phyllis and Mason really enjoyed it. I believe that for the first time I saw the eyes of Mason truly illuminated by the sun, which replaced to advantage the lights of the catheterization room.

We arrived in Verona with the night well advanced. Professor Besa was waiting for us. We stayed three days, one for the medical meeting and the other two for touring Florence and Venice. Phyllis loved the museums while I began to feel bored. In one of them, the window gave a splendid view of the countryside in all its colors that midday. I called Mason over and said to him: "You really believe that there is more beauty here inside than that you can see through the window?"

From Verona we went on to Rome for three days, where we had been invited by the University, and then on to Madrid to end our trip in the Clínica de la Concepción where Gregorio de Rábago and his colleagues played hosts to us.

During those three weeks we enjoyed our friendship immensely, but most importantly we had shared our knowledge with innumerable colleagues, always with the intention of benefitting the patient. Mason loved to watch me trying to give my talks in French, Italian and of course Spanish in the respective countries. It wasn't that I knew the French and Italian well. I had prepared my talks with the help of Hudon from Canada and Spampinato from Naples, two of our Residents at the time.

I would like to say something about my own experiences in trying to get my colleagues to understand that for the first time we had managed to develop a technique for rapidly improving the deficit of the coronary circulation. I had to argue with Burch, Friedberg, Likoff, McIntosh, Russek, and others who with their conservative spirit presented innumerable objections which came from earlier failed attempts to revascularize the heart without having adopted a solid base. In addition they did not have a clear idea of coronary cineangiography, despite it having been introduced ten years earlier. I was, for example, invited by the National Heart, Lung, and Blood Institute in Bethesda to present our surgical work. I soon realized that the language we used to describe the coronary circulation was not understood by them, and so asked for a blackboard on which I drew the two main arteries and their branches naming them properly so we could begin to understand each other. Most of the time I spent looking at and reading coronary cineangiograms. I found that the lack of knowledge of coronary anatomy and its implications for the myocardium, so vividly demonstrated in the films, constituted an important barrier. Despite the discussions becoming, at times, rather passionate, they never descended to the personal level and I always parted friends with my listeners, that had increased over the years. It is a source of great pleasure to me to meet my old friends, especially in the American and international congresses where almost always, after exchanging greetings, we start remembering the important stages of development of our specialty and also our disagreements and misunderstandings.

Naturally, I was invited to congresses and hospitals in Latin America. In Mexico I met the great maestro Chávez who was a co-founder of cardiology with Paul D. White, and in San Pablo in Brazil Professor Zerbini who was a pioneer of cardiovascular surgery in that country. In Argentina I took part in the congresses of the Argentine Society of Cardiology and the Argentine Federation of Cardiology and a few times performed operations at the request of my colleagues in the Italian Hospital and in the Güemes Hospital. I also took time to visit my family, even just for a few days.

Occasionally I had to join battle. I remember very well that it was in Buenos Aires where I had a serious encounter during the World Congress of Cardiovascular Surgery in 1968 with Professor Petrovsky, a prestigious Russian surgeon who was also Minister of Public Health. He presented resection of ventricular aneurysms, for which he first made a right thoracotomy to place the cannulas and then a left thoracotomy to expose the aneurysm, and in the majority of cases used a clamp of his own invention to occlude the base of the aneurysm which was then sutured from above. I thought of the clots which were almost always present in the cavity of the aneurysm and of the emboli (displaced clots) that could result. I stood up and said that this was no way to approach ventricular aneurysm in the present day and that the correct technique of dealing with them was to make a simple midline incision, connect the patient to the heart lung machine, open the aneurysm widely to evacuate the thrombi and precisely determine the size before resecting. The red-faced Professor began to ask me questions via the interpreter. The first:

"Who are you?"

Somewhat surprised I answered: "René Favaloro."

"Where do you work?"

"In the Cleveland Clinic in the United States of America."

"Do you speak from personal experience?"

It was time to make everything clear. I told him that if he looked in the literature he would find that we had the most important series in the world. I expanded my explanation of the surgical technique, analyzed our mortality rate which was infinitely lower than his, and emphasized the importance of revascularizing the coronary circulation involved as well as completing the aneurysmectomy so as not to do only half a job. He sat down without making a reply.

That afternoon I was operating in the Italian Hospital and when I had finished placing the sutures for a mitral valve replacement the anesthetist told me that I had a call from the Russian Embassy. I asked him to explain that I was operating. Professor Petrovsky wished to invite me to a reception at the Embassy that night. I accepted and went. On entering, I was surprised at the large number of guests. I was introduced to Petrovsky and on shaking hands with me he said smilingly to those around us "Here is my enemy." I was surprised for the second time that night. I explained to him that I was not his enemy and that, on the contrary, it was my custom to respect all my colleagues but that I felt that it was my obligation, given the presence of so many surgeons from around the world, to present my point of view which on this occasion did not coincide with his. I maintained that without free discussion of ideas it was impossible to advance.

Petrovsky had been invited to act as President of the next congress which was to be held in Moscow in two years, and he invited me to participate. We hugged each other and he called for vodka to be served. He toasted Argentina and I Russia. I took a small sip, never having been fond of alcohol. "No, no" he told me . "You must drink all of it as we do in Russia when we make a toast!" I felt obliged to do it.

Two years later I went to Russia for the first time, and at the cocktail reception held to open the congress I met Petrovsky who embraced me and said "Here is Dr. Favaloro.

He was my enemy!" He still remembered our discussion in Buenos Aires. He invited me to his hospital for the following day and told me we would have breakfast there.

When I arrived we sat with his colleagues at a long table loaded with caviar, eggs, sausages, hams, onions, and I don't know how many other items, together with bottles of vodka, cognac, wine and champagne. I am not exaggerating. We raised our glasses to anything and everything you can imagine: to his country, to my country, to his flag, to my flag, to his national anthem and to mine, to friendship, brotherly love, etc,etc,etc. At about ten in the morning Petrovsky asked us to rise and begin rounds in the hospital. On standing up my head was ready to explode, I felt dizzy and confused, sat down again and said that I would first need a bed. He replied that I could never become a member of his team!

After a short rest I was able to make rounds and analyze the patients who were presented to me, including one doctor. In future visits we continued to exchange ideas and I got to know other Russian surgeons and cardiologists such as Burakovsky, Chazov, Dolabjian, and Kolessev in Leningrad, who was a pioneer of the internal mammary-coronary anastomosis. His son worked at my side for four months in the Cleveland Clinic.

I have always thought that the work of the surgeon does not stop in the operating room. I feel that he has an obligation to transmit his knowledge through teaching in the broad sense of the word. His efforts should be concerned with the training of new surgeons, especially when he discovers someone with extraordinary qualities. He should act as a guide, placing himself on the other side of the table in the assistant's position. It is during these moments that he should feel happy to be able to share his knowledge. This is the secret of teaching. I confess that I have always felt, and continue to do so, an immense happiness difficult to describe when I see that I have been understood and that the motions in the operation are carried out with dexterity and security. A surgeon should hope that his spiritual sons - the Residents -will not only imitate him but surpass him in their creativity. This is the only way to progress, without egoism or unhealthy differentiation. That is how I did it in the Cleveland Clinic and how I do it in Argentina. Without exaggerating, hundreds of surgeons have learned at my side and are now dispersed through the world.

To them we can add the innumerable visiting surgeons from many countries who have come to see my work and have stayed for various periods of time, the majority of them having been in practice for years. There were so many that I had to limit the number to three at any one operation in order to avoid infection. I explained in detail what I was doing and slowed down the basic maneuvers. Following the operation while savoring tea we would continue with the explanations, almost always with sketches made on sheets of paper which they themselves would give me. In this way they would return home and generally after a short while would communicate the results of their first coronary operations.

If we add to this, publications, exhibits, movies, and my participation in many medical meetings of all shapes and sizes, you will see that I have always felt a tremendous passion for education. I have said on many occasions that when I am gone I would prefer to be remembered for my teaching rather than for my surgical activities.

4

The Final Years

In 1968 I performed my first heart transplant. As I
have mentioned, kidney transplants had been done for
some time in the Clinic and so there was already a team
experienced in the management of rejection, the Achilles'
heel of transplantation. In addition, the Immunology Section under Dr. Deodhar had developed an antilymphocytic
serum in horses kept on Dr. Crile's farm. Only four centers
possessed serum at that time. As a result I concluded that
if any center in the U.S. was to develop heart transplantation
then it surely must be the Cleveland Clinic. Effler and
Groves were indifferent towards the idea but Sones was
strongly opposed, arguing that we would stray from our
prime task, which was that of treating coronary patients. We
had heated discussions in B10 but there was no way of
persuading him. This aside, it still cost me a lot of work to
get the approval of the Surgical Committee, which was
necessary before presenting the project to the Board of
Governors. I spoke individually with each of its members to
gain their support and finally the project was approved.
From then on it was a question of looking for donors and

recipients. We selected a patient from Akron who was suffering from terminal myocardiopathy, a disease of the heart muscle fibers, and who was in chronic heart failure.

The biggest problem was to find a donor. The emergency room at the Cleveland Clinic only rarely received severely injured patients, so I got in touch with the neighboring hospitals. Almost all of them had doctors who had been trained in the Cleveland Clinic. So it was that early one morning I received a call from a former Resident, a neurosurgeon working at St. Vincent's Charity Hospital, who told me that a truck had fallen off a bridge joining two highways and that a woman accompanying the driver had suffered grave head injuries in the accident. She was alive at the present moment only because she was connected to a respirator. It was necessary to wait for her family to arrive from their home about a hundred miles from Cleveland so that they could sign the consent form, and to get the approval of a judge. The patient was finally transferred to our Intensive Care Unit.

That day I had to perform three operations, two of them combined procedures, and it was necessary to demonstrate that a transplant would not interfere with our daily activities. As I operated I received information from the Intensive Care Unit. Now and again the donor had arrhythmias and some episodes of low blood pressure, so I had to carry on with my work under the tension of possibly not getting to do the transplant. Viljoen, who was in charge of the anesthesia with Del Portzer, went to see our recipient and on his return he told me: "René, you are crazy. The patient is hardly breathing, he is cyanotic, and his arterial pressure is only just touching 90 as a maximum." I told him that it was precisely for this reason that the patient was a candidate for transplant and that an earlier study had shown that despite all his problems, his liver and kidneys continued to function well. I finished my last operation at about 5 p.m. I called together the team that had been working with me in the preparatory stages and each one repeated what he had to do. San Gupta, the chief Resident, was to remove the donor heart. In those days we did not have cardioplegic solution, which today we use to protect the heart muscle; the donor heart would be without blood flow from the moment of removal until the moment it was sutured to the recipient. Our tasks would have to be perfectly synchronized, which is why I insisted on the trial run. We would be working in adjoining rooms. At the last moment, Groves said to me, "René, would you like a hand?" I replied, "Naturally, and I thank you enormously."

Fortunately it all went off without a hitch. While San Gupta was opening the donor's thorax, I was doing the same with the recipient's; when I began the cannulation, he began the removal. I took out the diseased heart as rapidly as possible. I will always remember the strange sensation of looking at the empty pericardium. We spent exactly 45 minutes. On releasing the aortic clamp, blood began to flow freely through the coronaries and the heart began to beat. In a few minutes more the heartbeat was strong and we could disconnect the extracorporeal circulation. The patient was later sent to the Intensive Care Unit. Viljoen commented on the changes we saw. The blood pressure was now within normal limits, the skin was a rosy pink and warm, and the lungs appeared clear in the chest X-ray. All in all, it was just like any other patient.

We had tried to keep everything secret to avoid publicity. However, the news leaked out somehow and we found out through my wife, who called me, surprised, saying that she had heard about the transplant on television and wanted to know if it was true. I had been so busy that I had not called her during the day.

The morning after the operation the *Plain Dealer*, the Cleveland newspaper, carried a large photograph of Effler and attributed the transplant to him. We were worried by the amount of blood being lost via the thoracic drainage tubes.

The patient continued to bleed during the afternoon and even though his laboratory results lay within the normal range as the result of transfusing blood we decided to reopen him. We thought that a suture might be faulty. In this way we were able to see the heart again, beating vigorously. The blood came from a small branch of the right coronary in the anterior wall of the right ventricle, lacerated by the end of the pacemaker cable which we had placed as a precaution. A simple 4-0 suture stopped the bleeding and the patient recovered with no further problems.

The radio, television, and press continued to inform every day. To understand this you have to regress to 1968. It was the first successful transplant in the northeastern United States and it had been done in Cleveland. Effler continued to appear as being responsible for the transplant and this provoked unfavorable comments from various members of the Staff. I however was happy with this state of affairs. In some way it was a chance to thank him for having taught me and for having given me so much liberty and stimulation in my work. For example, I owed it to him that I had been accepted as a Fellow of the American College of Surgeons without possessing the required qualifications. I also owed him my membership of the American Association for Thoracic Surgery, the first time they had broken their rules about having the Board exam in the speciality which in turn depended on having the Board exam in general surgery. There is nothing worse than ingratitude, and this is often seen in young surgeons who, once they have begun to fly by themselves, tend to forget who it was who reared them.

A month later, on a Saturday morning just before sending the patient home, we held a meeting in the presence of the patient in the auditorium of the Education Building, presided over by Dr. Hoerr. No one stayed away and the auditorium was filled by the Staff, Residents, scrub nurses, nurses, technicians, etc etc. The meeting began with an introduction presented by Effler who between jokes recalled my first steps in the Cleveland Clinic. For example, he said that I had learned English by watching television which was why my English was so bad, and that I was better at barbecues than at surgery. He finally related my contributions and finished by saying that "at this moment the Board of Governors" - of which he was a member - "has a big problem. We don't know whether to continue calling this Clinic the Cleveland Clinic or the Favaloro Clinic." I felt like a drowned duckling in my seat, and my tears were evidence of my profound emotion. I got up and went to the podium and gave a detailed account of all we had done, thanking everyone involved and especially Effler. The patient, Mr. Lawson, lived for about two years. He died suddenly one cold morning as he was going to get the newspaper. I always thought that this was due to an excessive administration of diuretics that had been started the week before to combat the edema (swelling) resulting from the corticoids used to prevent rejection. It is well known that diuretics can cause an important loss of potassium and consequently provoke arrhythmias.

We performed only one more transplant, some months later, and the patient died after one month due to acute rejection. Unfortunately the program was not followed up. I still think that we lost the best opportunity of making the Cleveland Clinic the pioneering center for transplantation in the United States. We had everything we needed.

I remember that in the summer of '68 I painted the exterior of our house, which was largely built of wood. Toni and I had seen how the paint was deteriorating, especially in the front which faced north and received the full force of the snowstorms. Most of our neighbors painted their own houses and it appeared obvious that I should follow their example. With Jack's help I bought all the necessary materials, the most important being a long and solid ladder. What took the most time was the cleaning and sanding, especially the doors and windows where the old paint was peeling but still offered resistance. I worked every weekend and did not finish until the beginning of autumn, the area to paint being large despite the ease of use of roller paint brushes. The house looked whiter than ever, and I felt pride in my work.

During 1969 we continued to gain confidence in our work thanks to the careful observations made by Dr. Bill Sheldon, an associate of Sones, on our operated patients showing that they were evolving satisfactorily. William Proudfit, the chief of the Cardiology Department, had made significant contributions to our knowledge of the natural evolution of coronary disease. Bill, as we always called him, is an exceptional man of great humility. Besides his clinical tasks he is also a meticulous and organized observer who can pass hours and hours analyzing the data he collects patiently, with perseverance and above all absolute scientific honesty. I have no doubt of the great importance of his contributions concerning the evolution of coronary disease. He correlated the different clinical manifestations with the cineangiographic studies and showed that there was a direct relationship between the number of coronary lesions and the percentage narrowing of the vessels these caused and the state of the heart muscle. His work was monumental, involving the study of hundreds and hundreds of case histories. Today it is very easy for us to state that one-vessel disease is different from two-vessel or three-vessel disease, that narrowings of 20, 30, 50, or 70 percent make a significant distinction and that the heart muscle can be classified as normal, mildly, moderately, or severely affected. We owe our knowledge to Bill Proudfit who continues to attend the Clinic every day despite having retired and with whom I continue to exchange ideas and projects.

On the bases established by Bill we could see what was happening to patients of similar characteristics who were or were not operated on. As time passed it was possible to demonstrate with absolute clarity that the worse the disease, the greater the benefit of the surgery. The graphs were testimony to this. In December 1969 we were able to present the results from 570 operated patients at the sixth Annual Meeting of the Society of Thoracic Surgeons in Atlanta. For the first time we reported that in addition to the coronary arteries we could all see and palpate as they ran superficially in the heart, we had also found some patients to have coronaries which ran deep inside the muscle, principally the anterior descending branch of the left coronary.

It often happens in the life of the surgeon that he learns by sad experience in the operating room. I will never forget the day on which we operated on a relatively young patient with indication for a triple bypass and in whom I was unable to find the coronaries. I called Mason and as the patient was on extracorporeal circulation we were able to examine the heart thoroughly. I lifted the heart from the pericardial sac and told him that the coronaries we had seen in the movie were nowhere to be found and that he had perhaps got the wrong movie. He did not accept and so we reviewed the case history and the movie; Mason proved to be right. I returned to the operating room and performed only one bypass, in the distal segment of the anterior descending artery which was the only one I could find. The patient died 48 hours later due to the inability of this distal bypass to perfuse adequately the left coronary so severely damaged by the proximal lesions.

At the autopsy I carefully dissected the distribution of the left coronary circulation. I started from its origin in the aorta and found to my surprise that the anterior descending branch penetrated the muscle in the interventricular groove and the circumflex branches did the same in the lateral wall. We paid a high price to learn this. From then on when we encountered the same problem from time to time we could solve it using a technique developed for that purpose. In my presentation I remarked for the first time on the need to use

magnifying lenses to improve visibility and allow the performance of anastomoses in arteries of only one millimeter in
diameter with excellent results.

About 50 percent of the patients received single or
double mammary artery implants in addition to the bypasses. In this way we combined direct revascularization
using the bypasses with indirect revascularization using the
Vineberg technique and its variants. It was difficult for us to
abandon the implants which had given us so many good
results. The global mortality in the series analyzed was
5.4%, without excluding the more complicated patients
requiring the combined technique.

During my presentation in Atlanta I noted that the
surgeons were still preoccupied by the possibility of dilation
of the vein grafts and clot formation. In April 1970 at the
Annual Reunion of the American Association for Thoracic
Surgery in Washington, my presentation was dedicated to
the application of the bypass technique to the left coronary.
I insisted on the necessity of using magnifying glasses and
above all on the use of the "non touch" technique. Instead
of dissecting the coronaries from the surrounding epicar-
dium and fat, once the point for making the distal anastomosis was identified we made a small longitudinal incision
using a delicate scalpel first in the pericardium and then in
the artery itself with no dissection. This considerably eased
our work, especially the suturing which now found the
artery supported by surrounding tissue. This technique
greatly surprised the majority of our visitors, who first
dissected the coronary. In the same presentation I remarked
that even totally occluded distal coronary branches could be
entirely reconstructed using the bypass operation. Eleven
cardiovascular surgeons from different hospitals presented
their own experiences during the discussion. It was more
than pleasing to see that the technique was being dissemi-
nated. By June we had performed 1,086 operations, with a
mortality of four percent.

We made fewer Vinebergs and as a consequence the number of double, triple or quadruple bypasses increased; 196 by August with a similar surgical risk, 4.1 percent.

In the same year, 1970, as a consequence of the work of George Green in New York, who came very close to joining us in the Cleveland Clinic, we started making direct anastomoses between the mammary artery and the coronaries (Figure 6C). Instead of implanting the mammary according to Vineberg's technique, it was dissected in the same way and joined directly to the anterior descending coronary artery. George operated with a high-powered microscope and insisted that its use was obligatory. In one of our many meetings I asked him how long it took to become accustomed to using it. He answered between 120 and 140 hours in the laboratory. I thought that this method would never become popular, so I used my normal magnifying glasses (magnifying two to three times) to dissect a mammary artery and anastomose it to the anterior descending using the usual technique for a saphenous vein bypass. We later extended this to other branches of the left coronary. After I left the Clinic, Loop, who was one of the most capable - or perhaps the most capable - of the Residents who worked with me was able to show the excellence of the long-term results.

The same year my book entitled *Surgical Treatment of Coronary Arteriosclerosis* was published. It summarized all that had passed since 1962; it was enriched by an extensive introduction written by Dr. Effler. Many people asked me how I had found time to write the book, knowing my intense daily routine. The truth is that I collected data during the week and wrote on Saturdays and Sundays at home, generally in the kitchen. Why the kitchen? Because sitting there I could look up occasionally and enjoy the beauty of the back yard. I was entertained by the cardinals that lived all the year round in the garden and busily searched for food in the feeder we had hung in the apple tree near the kitchen.

From the many letters I received I could verify the impact of the book. In particular the writers thanked me for the chapters dedicated to anatomy and to interpretation of the coronary cineangiograms, so necessary for the understanding of this devastating disease.

An event which contributed significantly to the world acceptance of coronary artery surgery occurred in London in the same year, 1970, on the occasion of the sixth World Congress of Cardiology held in the Royal Festival Hall and Queen Elizabeth Hall. I was invited to participate in a symposium on coronary surgery together with Ray Heimbecker, Arthur Vineberg and Charles Friedberg. The organizing committee allocated us a rather small room. At the same time, 2 p.m., the main hall was occupied by a session which, although important, was not of such wide interest.

Over the preceding days I had sensed the enormous interest in our symposium, which was confirmed when I arrived with Vineberg an hour early to organize our slides. The room was packed, making it difficult to get to the podium. A few minutes before the start the aisles were occupied, and many colleagues were standing with their backs against the walls. When we sat down and were ready I noticed the fragile figure of Paul Dudley White who was standing in front of us. I could not believe that no one had stood up to give his seat to the Father of cardiology.

Moments before starting the doors were closed, and Heimbecker began his presentation concerning resection of the myocardium in acute infarction to a growing background of voices raised in protest by the large number who had been unable to enter. Finally they broke through the side doors and were precipitated into the room. Fortunately someone was able to rescue Paul D. White. This interruption brought the session to a halt. The secretary of the congress spoke to us and then announced that the session would be repeated that afternoon at six, which of course was senseless because in the first instance a discussion cannot be repeated and in the second, Friedberg was due to return to the U.S. that same afternoon. Be that as it may, the effect was to calm everyone and Heimbecker finished his presentation. Vineberg then spoke about his own results and finally Friedberg and I discussed coronary artery bypass surgery.

Charley was an excellent speaker who frequently joked during his talks, entertaining his listeners. On a previous occasion I had suggested to him that he had mistaken his true profession as a worthy rival to Bob Hope. In London I vividly remember him starting his talk with: "These surgeons are very special. When the heart has a hole in it they close it up, and when it does not they make one." Everyone laughed but when I presented the accumulated statistics from our Clinic the joking stopped, for Charley commented that he found it hard to believe that the mortality was so low. I said that it should be impossible to doubt our honesty, and that the doors of the Cleveland Clinic were open to anyone who cared to review our case histories to prove for themselves that our numbers were correct. Some did come, and were able to confirm that what I had said was indeed correct. That Congress had a big impact, because colleagues from all over the world could see what we were doing for our patients, not all of them but a selected group chosen carefully especially on the basis of coronary cineangiographic findings.

During this trip Donald Ross had invited me to operate on some patients in the National Heart Hospital; these were the first patients operated on in England. The majority of the great European surgeons attended these sessions, which for me constituted a heavy responsibility. They carefully observed every detail. I made the mistake of not having taken any of our group with me, not even a scrub nurse. The surgical technique was still relatively new and was unknown to the people of the National Heart Hospital.

In the first operation I opened the distal third of the right coronary and, as was my custom, placed a suture on each side of the incision so that by using a slight traction on them I could more easily place the rest. The scrub nurse or "sister" as they say there, on seeing an apparently discarded suture in the operating field pulled on it and ripped the coronary. I was fortunately able to repair it by elongating the incision more distally. I told her: "Please Sister, from now on when you see something lying loose in the field, do not touch it."

At midday, once the patient had been taken to the postoperative care unit we went with Donald and the visiting surgeons to an old 'pub' near the National Heart Hospital where we continued to comment on the various aspects of surgical technique in detail. On the first day when the waiter came to us Donald asked me what I wished to drink. Those who are close to me know that I very rarely drink alcohol. I thought about the second operation waiting for me that afternoon and replied: "A cold Coca Cola." An explosion of laughter followed and Donald explained: "Listen, René, this pub has been here for hundreds of years and they have never served non-alcoholic drinks. If it occurred to us to ask for Coca Cola I do not know how they would react. It is highly possible that we would be thrown out violently, probably through the window." I decided to ask for a beer.

We performed surgery until Monday of the following week and finished only a few hours before leaving for the airport. "Don't worry, René, I will get my chauffeur to take you in one of my cars and you will arrive in good time."

We said goodbye to each other at the door of the hospital where the chauffeur was waiting with a Bentley, its age being difficult to ascertain as is often true of English cars. We passed by the hotel where Toni was waiting with the luggage. Everything went well until halfway through the journey when the Bentley started to misfire and its speed dropped significantly. We stopped at the edge of the road, the chauffeur opened the hood and began to make a thorough check of the maze of cables while I looked nervously at my wristwatch. "Well, we will have to go more slowly but will get there on time," said the chauffeur with typical English equanimity. The last few miles were interminable as the Bentley progressively lost power. We ran to board the airplane, and started the journey back to Cleveland.

During the flight I slept fitfully and images mingled in my mind. One which kept returning was that of a soprano dressed in white, interpreting songs by Mahler against a black background which emphasized even more her extraordinary beauty. Her recital formed part of the social program prepared by the congress organizers. That night I was exhausted, for in addition to my talks I had operated with Donald until late. I intimated that I would prefer to stay in the hotel but he insisted that we go to the concert. Before it started, fatigue overcame me and I could barely hold up my head. When that woman appeared and flooded my ears with her sweet crystalline and exceptionally pure voice I was brought back to life; I could not take my eyes off her. It is one of my most beautiful memories, and from time to time I revive it by listening to Janet Baker on a disc which Candice, my secretary, who knew of the anecdote, presented to me before I left Cleveland.

The London Congress saw the participation of a numerous Argentine contingent. I had travelled to my country quite frequently over the previous years and participated in the national congresses there. On a number of occasions I had been asked about the possibility of my returning home.

In London the question was asked with greater insistence and for the first time I began to think that they might be right, and the idea of returning home began to germinate and slowly to mature. I kept on working earnestly and enjoying our house in Pepper Pike, to which we had added even more beauty with violet magnolias, the first to bloom in early spring, and new varieties of azaleas, rhododendrons and roses.

The decision was by no means easy. Toni offered some resistance: "We would have to begin all over again," she said to me. I thought: "My work in the United States has been worthwhile, more than anything for the large number of young surgeons I have taught and who will now lead the way. Nothing will happen if I now decide to return." So it was that little by little I convinced myself that I should accept the new challenge. One day in October after finishing work I went to my office and wrote my letter of resignation. In it I told Effler that this was to be my last year. Among other things I wrote:

Dear Dr. Effler,

...as you know, there is no real cardiovascular surgery in Buenos Aires. Patients are going every day to San Pablo and the United States. Some of them are rich enough to afford the trip, but some are coming under great financial strain (one patient sold his house in order to be able to make the trip). Some of them cannot even afford to think about coming. They die slowly but surely without the proper treatment.

Brilliant doctors are coming to this country for postgraduate education. After two or three years of excellent training, they return home to find only indifference. "The Masters" cannot accept new ideas. Some return to the United States, and some remain in a lethargic atmosphere surrounded by frustration.

Destiny has put on my shoulders once more a difficult task. I am going to dedicate the last one-third of my life to build a thoracic and cardiovascular center in Buenos Aires. At this particular time, the circumstances indicate that I am the only one with the possibility of doing it. The department will be dedicated, beside the medical care, to postgraduate education with residents and fellows, postgraduate courses in Buenos Aires and the major cities inside the country, and clinical research. As you can see, we will follow Cleveland Clinic principles.

Money is not the reason for my departure. If that would be the main issue, I would take into consideration the offers made constantly to me from different places inside the U.S.A. The main purpose is to develop a well-organized service where I can train surgeons for the future. Believe me, I would be the happiest fellow in the world if I could see in the coming years a new generation of Argentineans working in different centers all over the country able to solve the problems of the communities with high-quality medical knowledge and skill.

I know of all the difficulties involved because I had practiced before in Argentina. At age 47, the logical and realistic resolution would be to remain at the Cleveland Clinic. I know I am taking the difficult road. You might remember Don Quixote was Spanish. If I do not accept the position as Head of that department in Buenos Aires, I will be living the rest of my life thinking of myself as a good solid s. of a b. My conscience would constantly be telling me, "You chose the easy way"...

I left the letter on his desk and made my way home. I must confess that during the drive through those familiar streets I could not control myself and wept disconsolately. Two days later Effler wrote to me. Up until this moment we had hardly spoken and I would go as far as to say that we had tried to avoid each other. He accepted my decision:

Dear René ,

Your letter does not come as a surprise, but, nevertheless, it comes as a great disappointment to me. You have been a tremendous catalyst to the Department and to the Cleveland Clinic itself. In the short time that you have been with us, both as a Fellow and as a Staff member, your professional work and your tremendous drive has made an impact upon the Cleveland Clinic Foundation, and more than that, upon the specialty of thoracic and cardiovascular surgery itself. Needless to say, I am extremely proud.

I think you are doing the right thing and I don't have

to tell you that I will support you in every possible way from this end. It will be interesting to see if a surgical flower from Argentina that has been transplanted to Cuyahoga County can now be retransplanted back to its origin. There may be some rejection phenomenon that you will have to contend with, but I can only reiterate my total confidence in you and in your professional future...

...Your loss to the Cleveland Clinic will be tremendous and will be felt by many of us; nevertheless, we are all realistic enough to know that an institution of this type keeps going as eager and qualified young men await their chance to take our places. Whereas I have no illusions about getting another Favaloro, I can, in the next 10 years of my career, stimulate the young men who follow by daring them to attain Favaloro's record...

I sent copies of my letter only to George Crile and Mason Sones. Barney replied:

Dear René,

Your letter was not only important but beautiful. I have read it carefully, and find myself in full agreement with your conclusions. Your country is too beautiful to desert at a time when you are needed there.

On the other hand, it will be a great loss to the Cleveland Clinic and to me personally to have you leave the Department of Thoracic Surgery. As you know, I have always had the greatest admiration not only for your ingenuity and clinical proficiency but also for the cooperation that you have always shown with your colleagues. I will miss you very much...

Again may I express my regrets at your decision and my compliments for the moving reasons that have necessitated it.

I hope that the transcription of these paragraphs will be interpreted correctly. The references to my person and to my work in the Cleveland Clinic are a consequence of having worked from the very first day with responsibility, effort, dedication, honesty and humility, sharing with everyone the achievements we have reached. Neither vanity nor narcissism has a place in my soul. On the contrary I have always thought them to be bastard sentiments. I have included the transcripts 20 years later, so that it can be seen that my return did have a definite end that I believe has materialized with the passing of the years. This is evidenced by 300 graduates, principally from Argentina and Latin America, and by the Department of Research in our Foundation. The soon-to-be-opened Institute of Cardiology, Cardiovascular Surgery and Organ Transplantation, in which so many of our hopes have rested, will be the culmination of my task. I hope that all my readers, especially the younger ones, now understand.

The following week Effler and I met in his office and had a long talk. I told him that I had great hopes for the two senior residents, Loop and Cheanvechai, and that I would dedicate my time to leaving them well-prepared now that they would be operating on almost all my patients. I would be helping as always from the other side of the operating table. Effler communicated my decision to the Board of Governors and the chairman called me and asked me to reconsider my decision. He offered me a considerable increase in my salary, from 46 thousand to 65 thousand a year. I expressed my gratitude for his consideration but repeated that my decision was final. I did not particularly like Carl Wasmuth. I could never understand how he had become Chairman. From the time of my junior fellowship we barely tolerated each other. In one of the monthly clinical meetings we had argued so much that Dr. Hoerr had to abruptly terminate the session. The next day in his office he explained to me that I had been correct but must understand that I was a junior Fellow and Wasmuth the Chief of the Department of Anesthesia. I thanked him for having the courtesy to call me.

What I could not tolerate in Wasmuth was his contemptuousness. If a nurse anesthetist could not manage the intubation he would help her and then stroll out of the operating theater wearing an arrogant smile without even connecting the tube to the respirator. I have painted this picture of him because at the end of our conversation he said to me: "René, you must understand that if you go now the doors of the Clinic will be closed to you forever." I got up and answered: "That is your opinion. We will have to confirm it with the rest of our colleagues." I half turned and went out. A few years later it was he who had to go, in the middle of a commotion which went beyond the confines of the Clinic.

Weeks later Effler sent a memo to all Departments of the Clinic communicating my resignation and designating Loop as "Assistant Staff."

I manifested my total agreement with him. In the following years Loop would confirm the correctness of his nomination as Head of Department, where he demonstrated his management and leadership skills as well as his great surgical ability.

The news of my resignation and return to Argentina spread outside the Clinic and I was showered with proposals from different colleagues, among whom were some notable surgeons, as well as from various institutions offering me private practice which meant making fabulous sums of money. Some calculated around 2 million dollars a year without exaggeration. It would be necessary to operate on only two or three patients a day. They evidently did not know me well, for monetary interest has never been the motivation for my surgical practice. It was not in Jacinto Aráuz, nor had it been in the Cleveland Clinic where I had worked for a salary, and neither would it be in Buenos Aires where I was going principally due to my dedication to teaching.

The final months were very difficult to live out. Wherever I went the doctors, nurses, technicians, administrative staff, and even the porters asked me to stay on. One staff member even asked me if I realized that I was changing a Cadillac for a Model T. I replied that he should remember that the Model T was my country! The most difficult was to live with Mason. We continued to see patients together, some of whom I would operate on afterwards, and he never lost the chance of trying to convince me of what he saw as my error. He could not conceive of my abandoning our work in common. After ten years of working together there was a deep brotherhood between us. We had dreamed and made into reality ideas and projects during a very special period in modern cardiology, but circumstances had dictated that I leave.

Perhaps, and especially in the operating room, I appear to be a strong personality and to "have decided that not a hair on me shall move," as my countrymen would say. This is not the case, for deep in my soul I am extremely sensitive. I thought of how painful it was going to be to have to say goodbye to everyone, and decided to escape. We had planned that I would leave in the first days of July, but I deliberately accepted an invitation to speak in Boston in the middle of June and from there we travelled directly to Argentina. The only person who knew of my decision was Candice who kept her word to tell no one of this. I left letters for Effler and Sones in which I explained my decision. Effler replied that he was in agreement and that it helped to "avoid a painful goodbye or farewell," but Mason wrote to me saying once more that I was mad!

I left an important part of my life in Cleveland. My strongest impression is that I worked in an honest environment with absolute academic liberty and that our achievements were a consequence of our having been in reality a single family.

My departure was not a parting of the ways, for we continue to work together. The fight was still to be fought and there was still a long way to go. The randomized trials so long hoped for by the cardiologists yielded results which although in my view confirmed what we already knew, caused more confusion than enlightenment because they were organized dogmatically. In my frequent visits to the United States I did not hesitate to visit the Cleveland Clinic where we would get together again and exchange ideas. I had been able to reproduce in Buenos Aires a Department similar to that in the Cleveland Clinic and we continued to work in clinical investigation and teaching, and in time established a basic research section which has brought me a great deal of satisfaction. I thus had a lot of material to discuss and analyze, and our different sections have complemented each other most of the time. In 1977, the tenth anniversary of aortocoronary bypass was commemorated by the Clinic with a symposium to which were invited cardiologists and surgeons from the United States and various foreign countries. With emotion and pride I received the most important award bestowed by the Clinic: "Fellow of the Cleveland Clinic International Center for Specialty Studies."

In 1985 my wife and I made the most difficult trip. Mason had been operated on twice for lung cancer and although he had recuperated, the dissemination of the cancer was causing his health to deteriorate. In the middle of June I received a call from his secretary. She asked if I was going to be in Buenos Aires because Mason wished to visit me. I thought it was strange but happily responded yes, having no obligations to fulfill abroad at that time. The days went by without receiving another call to confirm the date of his arrival. I called his secretary who informed me that Mason was growing weaker and his wish was to see me one last time before he died. Unfortunately his condition had rapidly grown worse and he was now unable to travel. I talked it over with Toni and we decided to visit him. In reality I do not know how I summoned up enough courage.

We spent the weekend together. I found that he had deteriorated physically but still retained his brilliant and lucid mind. Friday and Saturday we were happy to be with each other again. He asked what new things I was doing in Buenos Aires and we recalled innumerable anecdotes, especially those concerning the clinical meetings in which we had fought side by side against incomprehension, and we remembered our trips together, and those outstanding three weeks in France, Italy, and Spain. "Remember, René, you spent the whole time eating prosciutto." His daughter, who had been at his side for the past few months, told me that my arrival had produced a notable change in him. On the Saturday night we dined with Shirey and Proudfit as we had done so many times in the past. Mason was good-humored and had a good appetite. It was a happy event, as though nothing bad was occurring.

Sunday was different. The happiness disappeared little by little. We ended with just the two of us sitting in a room together. We looked at each other in silence, and our view became clouded by the tears we both shed. I managed to say: "Well, let's not act like this. After all we will be seeing each other again one day in Heaven."

Mason replied: "You believe that, René? I have my doubts."

A long embrace while we continued to cry disconsolately was our last goodbye. He died on August 29, 1985. Mason has not truly died, he has gained a worthy place in the history of medicine and in cardiology in particular. He will always be remembered for his contributions which opened the doors to a new world through coronary cineangiography.

5

Historical Landmarks

I have related the principal events of my stay in Cleveland. I hope that this has served to show that the various achievements we managed to attain were a result of a team effort fundamentally on the part of the Department of Cardiology under the direction of Bill Proudfit, the Laboratory of Cineangiography with Mason Sones and collaborators, and the Department of Thoracic and Cardiovascular Surgery led by Effler, all with their minds firmly oriented towards the patient and how to benefit him. I do not deny that we had our disagreements, which were to be expected, but they were minor and did not interfere in the slightest with our prime objectives.

I have had to tell this story many times in the first person, having been one of the active participants contributing new ideas to the development of coronary surgery. Not to have told it like this would have been an excess of modesty which some of those who do not know me well would have commented on disparagingly. However, it should be clear that to me the individual does not count.

It is time to understand that "Me" has been replaced

by "Us." If my ideas have borne fruit it is because they germinated and grew in fertile ground to which all contributed. We were in reality a true family as I have already stated, not just the Staff but also the Residents, the nurses, the technicians, etc. All pulling together in the same direction.

It was indeed important to impress upon each one of them the transcendence of the work they were doing however insignificant it might appear. To do this it is necessary to get down from your horse and live with the members of the group, without losing the authority which does not come from the title or office which one bears but from what one shows through a combination of wisdom and dedication to the job. It costs nothing to give a little affection, to concern yourself with the problems each one might have in his daily life outside the hospital and try to understand and help if at all possible, of course without entering into demagogy. In this way any success becomes shared and one can feel it at any moment. I felt it in my soul every time something new was achieved because we were all happy irrespective of our different offices.

When I wrote my book on the *Surgical Treatment of Coronary Arteriosclerosis* in 1970, I investigated its history for the first time. I have to confess that I did not know most of the previous contributions written on the subject. My first observations were included in one of the chapters. From then on I accumulated more data which I presented in a paper published in the *International Journal of Cardiology* in 1983.

I later completed the information, which I have summarized as follows:

A. Experimental work

1. Alexis Carrel, 1910
This French doctor had begun to work in vascular

surgery in France in 1901 and later moved to New York where he continued his work in the Rockefeller Institute. In a communication to the American Surgical Association on March 5, 1910 he presented the first experimental studies on aortocoronary bypass using segments of carotid artery. He stated:

" In some cases of angina pectoris, when the origin of the coronary arteries is calcified, it would be useful to establish a complementary circulation by way of the distal part of the arteries. I tried to make an anastomosis between the descending aorta and the common left carotid artery. For many reasons it was a difficult operation. Due to the continuous movement of the heart it was by no means easy to dissect and suture the artery. In one case I anastomosed one end of a long cold-preserved carotid in the descending aorta. The other end was passed through the pericardium and anastomosed to the peripheral part of the coronary, near the pulmonary artery. Unfortunately the operation was very slow. Three minutes after interruption of the circulation the heart fibrillated but the anastomosis took five minutes. On massaging the heart the dog came alive but died two hours later. This experiment demonstrated that the anastomosis must be made in less than three minutes."

He could generally perform a vascular anastomosis in five minutes using the techniques that he had developed. He had learned some of the details by watching an embroiderer! Alexis Carrel was undoubtedly the founder of vascular surgery. In addition he performed experiments at the beginning of this century on renal and heart transplantation. He was awarded the Nobel Prize in 1912.

2. Gordon Murray and collaborators

Murray was an extraordinary Canadian surgeon whom I had the immense pleasure of knowing personally. When I was invited as a visiting professor I heard from his own lips the story of his principal works during a tour of the museum of the University of Toronto where his innumerable contributions in the most diverse fields of surgery are conserved.

His studies were made in the Caven Memorial Research Institute, of which he was Director. In 1940 in *Archives of Surgery* he reported on his experimental work on resection of portions of coronary arteries and their replacement using various segments; "the objective is to explore the possibility of resection of the calcified and stenotic portions and their replacement with a graft to improve the circulation."

In 1951 in a presentation to the New York Academy of Medicine he referred to his experimental work on implantation of the mammary artery - later continued by Vineberg - and the resection of acute infarcts which improved the function of the left ventricle, applied in humans by Heimbecker years later.

In the second Congress of the International Society for Angiology in Lisbon in September 1953 he presented the first experimental study of direct anastomosis between the internal mammary artery and the coronary circulation. To do this he ingeniously introduced a small tube via one of the lateral branches of the mammary artery which he then advanced distally and introduced into the selected coronary artery via a small incision to irrigate the territory. He could thus prevent interruption of the blood supply and consequent infarct while joining the two arteries.

In December 1954 in the *Journal of the Canadian Medical Association* he reported his experimental studies on coronary bypass with arteries, using the internal mammary, the subclavian, the axillary, and the carotid which he considered to give the best results. It is important to reproduce his final comments: " It will be necessary to know previously if the coronary artery is permeable and in good conditions in the segment distal to the proximal obstruction.. In order to have this information, angiography must be employed either in the Radiology Department or in the operating room. The injection of a radio-opaque substance into the coronary artery will show the state of its caliber. It will not only present the challenge of diagnosing the stenosis but also permit us to see the state of the proximal and distal portions..When we have this information we will have the possibility in appropriate cases of obtaining more precise information on the function of the coronary arteries."

We had to wait for four years before Sones made this overriding necessity into reality.

It is important to point out that these experiments were made possible by the use of heparin, discovered in 1937, which prevented the formation of blood clots, so often the cause of previous failures.

3. Richard T. Mamiya and collaborators, 1961

In the University of Saint Louis Mamiya made end-to-end anastomoses between the left subclavian artery and the left coronary artery, and at the same time anastomosed the left internal mammary artery to the right coronary. In reality Mamiya did this work with valve replacements in mind.

4. Lester R. Sauvage and collaborators, 1963. Providence Hospital, Seattle, Washington

Sauvage et al used the external jugular vein as a bridge between the descending aorta and the circumflex branch of the left coronary. He operated on 46 dogs with a high incidence of occlusions, and observed in non-occluded dogs that the vein was dilated. As a result use of the saphenous vein was suggested due to its thicker wall and more appropriate size.

5. Akiyo Wakabayashi and John E. Connolly, 1968. University of California, Irvine, California

In a paper read at the annual meeting of the American Association for Thoracic Surgery, they reported on a comparative study of blood flows in a segment of internal mammary artery used as a bridge between the ascending aorta and the circumflex artery, and segments of saphenous vein (mentioned for the first time in experimental work) between the ascending aorta and the anterior descending and circumflex branches of the left coronary artery.

B. Clinical application of aortocoronary bypass

1. David C. Sabiston Jr., Duke University Medical Center, Durham, North Carolina

On March 22, 1974 in the William F. Rienhoff Lecture given in the Turner Auditorium of the Johns Hopkins Medical School Sabiston related that on April 4, 1962 in a patient in whom he had previously performed an endarterectomy (extraction of atheromatous plaques from the internal and medial layers of an artery) he constructed a saphenous vein bypass from the ascending aorta to the distal segment of the right coronary artery. The patient died three days later due to a cerebral complication, presumably arising from the thrombi found at autopsy in the proximal anastomosis. As a result, he stopped using saphenous vein bypasses until he became aware of the results of the group at the Cleveland Clinic.

2. H. Edward Garrett and collaborators, 1964. Baylor College of Medicine, Houston

In the *Journal of the American Medical Association* of February 12, 1973, Garrett reported that on November 23, 1964 he constructed an aortocoronary bypass to the anterior descending branch of the left coronary artery, with the assistance of S. Pitzell, M.K. Neugenbauer, and L.C. Zange. The original objective of the operation had been to effect an endarterectomy followed by reconstruction using venous patches in an obstruction compromising the distal extreme of the main left coronary and its branches.

Towards the end of 1970, Garrett told Effler that the patient had survived the operation. Donald told me of his conversation with Ed and I said that it would be of great value to locate the patient and restudy him to see if the bypass remained permeable. We would thus have a valuable indication of the long-term evolution of the bypass. Effler wrote to Garrett and the patient, who was 42 years old at the time of the operation was admitted for a new study. On September 9, 1971 it was shown that the bypass was still open and had suffered no modification. The operation by Garrett was without any doubt the first successful operation using the technique of aortocoronary bypass with the saphenous vein. However, I think it fair to point out that in Houston in 1964, which is where Garrett worked at the time, this was not considered important. They continued using the Vineberg technique, even experimenting and employing clinically with poor results the use of saphenous vein segments between the descending aorta and the left ventricle, where the distal end of the vein was implanted into a tunnel as a variant of the Vineberg technique. This is certified by publications appearing after the year 1964.

In mid-1968, as a consequence of the cumulative results of the Cleveland Clinic, in Houston they began to use the aortocoronary bypass technique as is documented by George Morris in the *Annals of Surgery*, October 1970. The results from 161 patients are analyzed up to April 1970. In this paper we read: "A point of significance to us has been the common finding at operation of a patent vessel beyond areas of complete occlusion which fail to visualize with preoperative arteriography." The answer is found in the same contribution: "Improvement in arteriography is needed and I think this will develop with technical improvements and experience." That the quality of cine coronary angiograms was inadequate in Houston is, to a large extent, a confession. By that time, because of the work of Sones and collaborators we were able at the Cleveland Clinic to see the coronary arteries in detail, including collateral circulation. Up to April 1970 more than 1,000 patients were operated in our clinic.

I remember that towards the end of 1968 I went to Houston after attending the annual meeting of our Society because I was interested in methods for assisted circulation. In an informal meeting I presented our results and followed this with a movie showing preoperative coronary cineangiographs, scenes from the operations, and the post-operative cineangiographs. The only comment came from Cooley who stood up and said, without much enthusiasm, "René, you have got something between your hands, continue with the good work." I had hoped for a more positive response.

When the Cleveland Clinic organized the symposium to celebrate the first decade of aortocoronarty bypass, guests were invited from various cardiovascular surgery centers including some from Europe. George Morris was the representative from Houston and began his dissertation by saying "Well, you are celebrating the tenth anniversary. We in reality are celebrating the thirteenth." I thought of the famous expression that "there is nothing better or bigger outside of Texas."

I repeat, these are anecdotes of little value.

3. Donald Kahn, 1971. Madison, Wisconsin
In April 1971 in the discussion following a presentation by Effler to the American Association for Thoracic Surgery Kahn said that he had operated on two patients, the first in March 1966 (bypass to the right coronary artery).

4. The Cleveland Clinic group, 1967 onward
These contributions have been discussed extensively in this book.

5. W. Dudley Johnson, 1968

This surgeon from the Marquette School of Medicine in Milwaukee, Wisconsin, must be considered one of the principal pioneers of myocardial revascularization surgery. Although he started in February 1967 with Vineberg's operation, by the end of that year he had operated on his first patients using the venous patch technique. In 1968 he went on to use the bypass technique.

His first report, "Agressive Treatment of Coronary Disease," was presented at the annual meeting of the American Association for Thoracic Surgery on April 1, 1969, when he analyzed 245 patients of whom 71 had received aortocoronary bypasses.

Following this, the emphasis on placing the distal anastomoses in the peripheral segments of the coronary arteries and the use of multiple bypasses in patients with diffuse lesions have been two of his fundamental contributions.

From the first years we have shared innumerable American and foreign congresses and fought side by side to impose the new techniques of myocardial revascularization. Our friendship has grown firm over the years. When he found out about my resignation, he suggested that we could work together anywhere in the United States instead of my returning to Argentina.

C. Experimental work on mammary coronary anastomosis

1. Gordon Murray, 1953
Previously discussed.

2. Alan Thal and collaborators, 1956. University of Minnesota
Performed experimental work anastomosing the left internal mammary artery to the circumflex branch of the left coronary and showed that the operation had a 75 percent

success rate, and that the arteries remained permeable up to six months which was the maximum duration studied. They suggested that this technique could be used clinically in the future.

3. Karel B. Absolon and collaborators, 1956
Repeated the above-mentioned work in the University of Minnesota, demonstrating the technique but did not make any long-term studies.

4. Edwin L. Carter and Earl J. Roth, 1957. Naval Medical Institute, Bethesda, Maryland
Communicated the possibility of making anastomoses without using sutures, by employing polyethylene rings to anastomose the internal mammary artery to the circumflex artery.

5. Robert H. Goetz and collaborators, 1960. Albert Einstein College of Medicine, New York
Used a similar technique, employing tantalum rings. Many communications reported systems for avoiding sutures, including the use of staplers, from Canada, Russia, and Japan. Despite having demonstrated their feasibility in experimental settings, these devices have not been clinically successful because they can only be used for end-to-end anastomoses, which requires that the coronary artery be transected to join its distal end to that of the internal mammary artery. In addition, the characteristics of diseased arteries are totally different from the normal ones of experimental animals.

6. Frank C. Spencer and K. Prachuabmoh, 1964. University of Kentucky Medical School
Work based on the techniques of microsurgery published for the first time in 1960 and developed by Julius H. Jacobson and Ernesto L. Suarez, utilizing delicate instru-

ments, and which have had a large impact on vascular surgery in general and coronary surgery in particular.

They reported their experiments on 16 dogs operated on with extracorporeal circulation, 7-0 silk sutures, and miniature scissors and needleholders. Immediate and long term results were excellent, and the operations were performed without the use of magnifying glasses or microscope.

It is my understanding that this was the first detailed description of the technique we use today with only minimal changes.

I have a longstanding friendship with Frank since he came to watch me work in the Cleveland Clinic in 1968, having been named chairman of the meeting at which my forthcoming first presentation would be made (annual meeting of the American College of Surgeons). This demonstrates once more the responsibility with which he has always acted. He called me from New York and said; "René, don't get annoyed if I come to Cleveland for a few days to see what you are doing. The College has named me chairman of your conference and it seemed logical to get to know your work in vivo and in detail." His visit was of great help to me.

After my conference came the questions. One was: "You do not use magnifying lenses. What diameter do the smallest arteries have in which you make naked-eye anastomoses?" "A millimeter, a millimeter and a half," I replied. A generalized murmur filled the hall, indicating that this reply was difficult to accept. Frank then said "That is absolutely true. I have seen it for myself watching Dr. Favaloro at work." Years later, as part of my historical investigations I discovered that Spencer himself did it in dogs in 1964.

7. Vasily I. Kolessov, 1965. Pavlov First Medical Institute, Leningrad

Performed internal mammary - coronary anastomoses with the help of magnifying lenses and a special cannula to avoid interruption of coronary bloodflow. He included angiographic studies in animals that had survived for one year and showed excellent results.

D. Clinical application of internal mammary artery

1. Robert H. Goetz and collaborators, 1960

On May 2, using as a basis his previous experimental studies, he performed an anastomosis of the right internal mammary artery to the right coronary using a tantalum ring.

2. Vasily I. Kolessov, 1966

As a result of his experimental studies he operated on six patients, five with anastomoses to the anterior descending artery and one to the circumflex. One patient died. The patients were operated on without prior angiography and with the use of magnifying lenses. His communication (November 15, 1966) was published in the *Journal of Thoracic and Cardiovascular Surgery*.

On one of my visits to Russia (1970) I went to Leningrad. Kolessov's son Eugene had worked with us for some months in Cleveland and I had been invited to see what they were doing in the Pavlov Institute. There I met his father, a simple and humble man of great surgical dexterity, and talked with one of the first patients operated on with young Kolessov as interpreter. They still operated on the majority of patients without cineangiography (they were about to install the equipment). The patients were selected on the basis of their clinical state and with the help of dozens of electrocardiograms recorded with a special technique which, I was told by the chief of the Electrocardiography Department, was capable of detecting badly perfused myocardial territories.

3. Charles P. Bailey and Terno Hirose, 1968. New York

In two patients studied using the Sones technique of cineangiography and lenses of two and one half times magnification, they anastomosed the right internal mammary and right coronary using interrupted sutures.

4. George E. Green and collaborators, 1968. New York University Medical Center

Following 42 experiments in dogs and using a microscope magnifying 16 times they anastomosed the left internal mammary artery to the anterior descending artery in two patients (February 29 and March 12). George undoubtedly should be recognized as the principal force behind the use of the internal mammary artery. In those days when the rest of us were using the saphenous vein George Green thought that the internal mammary artery would give better results. The long-term studies, especially following eight to ten years, showed him to be right. Today, the internal mammary arteries are justifiably considered to be a first choice for revascularization.

5. Cleveland Clinic, 1970

I knew of Green's work because we saw each other frequently in the medical meetings so common in the United States. When I asked him how long it would take to become accustomed to the microscope he replied no less than 120 to 140 hours in the laboratory. I thought that this technique would never become popular.

In the middle of 1970 I dissected the left mammary artery as usual and prepared the distal end, freeing surrounding tissue, and after making a small five or six millimeter incision in the proximal third of the anterior descending artery. I made the anastomosis using 7-0 sutures with the aid of my normal reading glasses. The operation ended without incident and the postoperative catheterization showed that the anastomosis functioned correctly. We thus began to employ this technique and extended it to other branches of the coronaries.

Maybe it is worthwhile to point out that in 1968 I performed a successful mamary coronary anastomosis (right mamary to right coronary artery) due to David Fergusson's insistence. Every time we were watching together a postoperative cineangiogram of a Vineberg approach he would say to me: "René, I know you can obtain the same connection in the operative room instead of waiting at least six months." Nevertheless it was difficult to abandon the Vineberg technique that gave us so many satisfactions.

Following my return to Argentina, Floyd Loop carried this work forward and the resulting publications in which the simplicity of the technique was evident allowed it to be adopted in many centers of cardiovascular surgery.

All of this has served to show that the idea of the aortocoronary bypass is an old one, originating as long ago as the beginning of this century with the work of Alexis Carrel. Once more we see how medical progress is a step-by-step process of evolution through innumerable contributions. It is very dangerous to say "I was first"; there is almost always a precedent.

The only merit of our team is to have worked continuously from 1962 in the global analysis of coronary disease on solid foundations, as a consequence of coronary cineangiography introduced by Sones in 1958. We have never claimed, though we could have, any priorities. Our satisfaction is that of having contributed, through sharing everything by our educational policy, to the improvement of the expectancy and quality of life of millions of persons. Aortocoronary bypass like any other therapy is only a palliative for coronary arteriosclerosis; this underlines the necessity of careful selection of the patients.

I cannot finish without expressing my concern, especially after the introduction of coronary angioplasty by Andreas Gruenzig in 1977, about the mercenary turn our profession seems to have taken. Medicine has not been able to escape the materialistic influence of the society in which we live, where possession and power appear to be the main objectives. Certain presentations in prestigious international meetings and publications in respectable medical journals do not resist the meekest scientific analysis based on serious and thoughtful grounds, including some randomized trials influenced by dogmatic ideas in the planning stage. Sometimes it appears that the surgeons, cardiologists, and those who practise angioplasty are each defending their economic wellbeing instead of honestly confronting the different therapies so that they can give the best advice to their patients. I believe the time has come to act if we wish to maintain the ethical basis of our profession.

We continue to live with passion. Only the passionate can perform lasting and fertile works, and we must not cloud our vision with veils of gold which we cannot take with us on the final journey. We will be accompanied only by the satisfaction of having done our duty well.

Colophon

> " *To sacrifice oneself in the service of life*
>
> *is to enjoy a state of grace.* "

A. Einstein

When I wrote this book I kept thinking all the time on the young generations of physicians that follow us. I hope after reading it, besides the history of myocardial revascularization, they will collect some seeds that will grow in their souls in a difficult moment of our society that has become extremely materialistic. It is important for them to find out as Henry D. Thoreau said in 1854 that it is not easy to "buy a blankbook to write thoughts in; they are commonly ruled by dollars and cents", and realize that "A grain of gold will gild a great surface, but not so much as a grain of wisdom."

Our profession is the most beautiful, sacrificed and compromised because it deals with human beings all the time, human beings that are suffering to recover their healths. It is mandatory in medicine to follow strict ethical rules.

Several years ago I wrote the following commandments to serve as guides to the members of our Foundation:

1. Honesty.
2. Work with passion, effort, and unlimited self-sacrifce.
3. Avoid being influenced by personal dogmas and prejudices or those suggested by others.
4. An individual's contribution will be of value only if it arises from his free will, exercised without external influences or limitations.
5. Never stray from a strictly ethical attitude, which implicitly is based on moral sense and on respect for the dignity and human condition of the patient and his family.
6. Teamwork is vital. This requires humility. The development of science has demonstrated that the actions of individuals should be subject to the common good and that the use of "I" has long been replaced by the use of "We."
7. Every action should be directed towards the truth and nothing more than the truth. It is important to speak out loudly one's inner thoughts. Nothing is gained by constructing on a basis of lies.
8. If, in addition to relieving the suffering of our fellow-man, we can enrich our knowledge then our satisfaction will be double.
9. Our work is centered on the patient. Consequently he is the only person who deserves priviliges.

10. The accomplishment of our work can only be enjoyed
    when we realize, preferably in those silences reserved
    for personal reflection, that the only true prize for us is
    that arising from the spiritual pleasure of duty well
    done.

I believe they can be extrapolated to all the physicians
and to some extent to the youths of our time. I have to
confess that I am extremely worried about them. Because of
my academic commitments I have had to travel all over the
world in the last twenty five years and I see that most of them
are spoilt by our consumer society. For them it seems to be
that power and money are the main issues. A good number
do not want to have any responsibility either with themselves, their families or our society. I believe this is the main
reason why they try to escape by following the road of drug
addiction. Where are their illusions and utopias? Are they
really satisfied? I do not think so.

Maybe they could listen to Louis Pasteur, the famous
French researcher who changed our knowledge mainly on
infectious diseases more than anybody else even though he
was not a physician. In a ceremeony to celebrate his
seventieth anniversary at La Sorbonne on December 27,
1892 he said: " Youth ! Youth ! confide in these reliable and
powerful methods of which we know nothing more at
present than the first secrets. Whatever your career may be,
do not succumb to denigrating and sterile scepticism, do not
become dispirited by those sad hours through which a
nation might pass. Live in the serene peace of the laboratory
and library. Ask yourselves at the beginning 'What have I
done to advance my vocation?'; later, as you advance, 'What
have I done for my country?' until the moment that you
attain, perhaps, that immense happiness of believing that
you have contributed something towards the progress and
good of Humanity. However Life may reward your efforts,
when the final moment nears you must be able to say to
yourself 'I have done all that has been within my power '."

It would be important for all of you, young people, to ask frequently: "What have I done for my development ?", I would suggest also that they think: "What have I done for the other members of our Society ?", because to practice one's profession is not enough. It should be a must to feel our responsibility towards all our fellowmen and help them, with strong participation in the main issue of our time that will be solved only by education. We can and it should be mandatory to enlarge our scope besides our principal work.

When I was a student at the University of La Plata, in Argentina, we learned that the projection of the University at the community level was part of our duties after graduation and certainly an obligation for all of us throughout our entire lives.

I hope you understand my feelings and have found through some of the comments I include in this book that the dream of one of my teachers in college, Pedro Henríquez Ureña: "America Land of Justice" (he was mainly thinking on Latin America) is still a dream that will come through only if we are morally committed to participate. It is difficult to deny that still now, even though we witness a tremendous technological development, millions of people are living in hunger and poverty without medical protection and unable to reach proper education.

The idea of a unified America that was always present in our history is a subject that is analyzed more frequently at all levels in our days, but it is important to emphasize that if we are going to be together, the main subject should be a search for justice. Certainly freedom is not enough. It will be important to detect the members of our Society who "will continually thrust their own low roof, with its narrow skylight, between you and the sky, when it is the unobstructed heavens you would view." It is time to: " Get out of the way with your cobwebs; wash your windows." (H.D. Thoreau, Life without Principle). It is time to participate. It is time to help. It is time to feel our responsibility.

Then, I hope once more you realize I did not write this book only to talk about myself, which would be totally dishonest and against my way of living. I worked with passion as part of a team. I still do and I will feel totally rewarded if you can read "between the lines" and find out that: "Two things fill my soul with admiration and an incessantly renewed respect, the starry heavens over my head and the moral law in the depths of my heart" (Emmanuel Kant).

I tried to follow the landmarks I received from my father (a carpenter) and my mother (a dressmaker) who taught me that honesty, dedication and effort were mandatory if I wished to accomplish something in life.

I expect everybody will realize at the end that I always tried -as Martínez Estrada taught me in College- to leave the place I live in cleaner and more beautiful than I found it. This will be enough after my departure.